Collective Bargaining by National
Employees in the United Kingdom

COMPARATIVE STUDIES IN PUBLIC EMPLOYMENT LABOR RELATIONS

Collective Bargaining
by National Employees in the
United Kingdom

RAYMOND LOVERIDGE
LONDON GRADUATE SCHOOL OF BUSINESS STUDIES

ANN ARBOR
INSTITUTE OF LABOR AND INDUSTRIAL RELATIONS
THE UNIVERSITY OF MICHIGAN—WAYNE STATE UNIVERSITY
1971

This monograph is one of a series prepared under the direction of Professors Russell A. Smith and Charles M. Rehmus of The University of Michigan, and is a part of their comparative international study of labor relations in public employment. Financial support of this research project has been derived from a number of sources. Basic grants came from the comparative law research funds of The University of Michigan Law School; the Institute of Labor and Industrial Relations, The University of Michigan—Wayne State University; the comparative economics research funds of The University of Michigan Economics Department; and the research programs of the New York State Public Employment Relations Board and the United States Department of Labor.

1/8/73 - 5.00

Contents

Collective Bargaining by National Employees in the United Kingdom

·I·

The Structure and Content of Collective Bargaining in the U.K.

COLLECTIVE bargaining provides the major institutional means to the determination of wages and conditions in British industry. About 18 million of a work force of approximately 24 million are affected by negotiations between management and organised labour. It is estimated that of over 16 million manual workers in employment, about 14 million are covered by such machinery, while less than 4 million of the 7.5 million nonmanual employees are affected.

The formal structure of the system is focussed upon negotiations which take place at the national level between associations of employers operating within a single industry or industrial sector and national trade unions acting individually or in confederations. Above this level is the permanent federal body of the trade union movement, the Trade Union Congress (TUC), replicated on the employers' side by the Confederation of British Industries (CBI), which is a representative of both trade associations and employer associations. These latter two bodies form most important pressure groups upon national government. Since the last World War their roles have been greatly extended by the existence of a whole range of post-Keynesian planning committees and other bodies with advisory or executive responsibilities for the administration of the welfare state.

In these activities the CBI and TUC have little de jure power to represent their members. As a result both have been forced to develop their internal communications with affiliated organisations to an unprecedented extent. In spite of this the sheer range of national business in which these bodies are engaged implies that an increasing amount of de facto power escalates to their national representatives. Yet underlying the basis for their participation in the process of national government is the permanency of the institutions they represent and the wide coverage of their membership.

EMPLOYER ASSOCIATIONS

The majority of the existing employer associations came into existence between the years 1890 and 1920. The latter year saw the formation of the British Employers Confederation which in 1965 merged with the two existing national trade associations to form the CBI. Though many local associations were in existence during the early nineteenth century, none had the permanency or sought to control conditions of employment over a geographical area greater than their immediate locality or region. There are some 750 autonomous employer associations in existence today of which only 104 are affiliated with the CBI. For the most part each of these seeks to control wage rates and conditions of employment applying within a single industry or industrial sector and represents anything between 50 to 90 percent of employers within its respective industry. The CBI claims to represent firms employing over 75 percent of labour in private industry and transport.[1] It can be estimated that in 1959 some 70 percent of these employees were covered by no more than 59 of the currently affiliated employer associations; the degree of concentration within a few associations such as engineering (metal manufacturing union) and printing is certainly greater than this. Since that time most of the state-owned corporations in railways, gas, electricity, and the post office have become affiliated to the CBI. On the other hand, several of the largest individual employers in the country, including many foreign-owned firms, have either broken with their industry's employer association or have refused to join. Some have remained individual affiliates of the CBI but have rejected their individual association's attempt to provide a substantive or procedural framework suitable for a whole industry inclusive of the very high proportion of small employer members as well as themselves.

TRADE UNIONS

At the end of 1968 just over 10 million British workers, or about 40 percent of the total employed population, were

1. CBI, *Evidence to the Royal Commission on Trade Union and Employers Associations,* Confederation of British Industries, November 1965.

members of trade unions. Of these nearly 9 million were in organisations affiliated to the TUC. Many more still were in quasi-professional or other occupational associations which entered into some intermittent bargaining activity on behalf of their members. A conservative estimate placed the number of trade unions in existence at that time at 534, of which only 155 were affiliated to the TUC. The multiplicity of unions is an historical feature of British industrial relations, but the obverse of this image is the concentration of over half the TUC's affiliated membership in eight large unions. Of these the three largest, the Transport and General Workers Union, the Amalgamated Engineering and Foundry Workers Union, and the General and Municipal Workers Union, comprise well over a third of total union membership.[2]

Unlike the employer associations, few unions are organised on an industrial basis. Of those that are, many are in declining industries—coal mining, textiles, railways, iron and steel manufacture—and tend to be losing members through the effects of technological innovation. Only in the public services, especially the post office and nonmanual civil and local government officers, are industrially based unions maintaining or increasing membership in the long term. The most successful unions appear to be those prepared to organise across industrial (both private and public) boundaries and also vertically across occupational boundaries. As a result the industry or plant-based employer often faces a number of unions. Sometimes these will represent a horizontal range of occupational groups, but equally often at least the major participants will be organising across several occupations within a single plant.

With the help of enabling action on the part of the government, who in 1964 amended the conditions under which union mergers (or "transfers of engagements") might take place, and with the help of the TUC in arranging post-merger conferences, the number of unions in existence has diminished considerably and continues to do so. There is nothing, however, in the pattern of present mergers to suggest that an industrial format

2. These data extracted from "Membership of Trade Unions in 1968," *Employment and Productivity Gazette*, LXXVII:11, November 1968, HMSO; also *Report of the 101st Annual Trades Union Congress, September 1969*, TUC, 1969.

will emerge, or even one which will reduce interunion competition. The craft or occupational union appears to be rapidly giving place to a prototypical general union in which industrial or job interests are represented internally within a unitary external identity.

Long term changes in the occupational structure have had an impact on trade union structure and, slowly, upon their recruitment policies. There has been a decline in the number of manual workers employed in the traditional industries, particularly in the primary producing industries. The sectors of employment which have expanded fastest since World War II have been education, professional and business services, insurance, banking and finance, and distribution, areas which have been largely neglected by the unions affiliated to the TUC. Yet even within declining industries the rate of growth among those in clerical and technical occupations, which have been largely ignored by manual unions, has been greater than the rate of decline among manual employees.

As a result the combined membership of affiliated unions expanded by only 11 percent between 1948 and 1964 and actually declined by 2.5 percent as a proportion of the employed labour force. This average overall expansion resulted almost wholly from a significant increase in the affiliated membership of a mere 43 purely white-collar unions affiliated to the TUC. The recent affiliation of the National Local Government Officers Association (1970 membership 370,000) in 1964 and the decision of the National Union of Teachers (240,000 members) to seek affiliation in 1970 provided much needed impetus in these areas. In general, however, the white-collar sectors have remained relatively unorganised compared with existing manual occupations. Professor George S. Bain has suggested that in 1964 only 29 percent of the total number of white-collar employees were organised compared with 51 percent of manual employees.[3] Despite the large increase in membership recorded by white-collar unions it appears that the rate of unionisation

3. George Sayers Bain, "The Growth of White-Collar Unionism in Great Britain," *British Journal of Industrial Relations,* IV, November 1966, 304-35.

among these occupations is barely keeping up with the growth in numbers entering them. If these rates of progress are maintained, the total level of unionisation within British industry must decline in the long run. With this fact in mind, many of the largest manual unions have reformed their internal structures over the past two years and have entered into the recruitment of white-collar employees with a new-found vigour. At the time of writing the TUC has been given little opportunity by the constituent unions to chart the direction of this new drive.

PROCEDURE AND CONTENT OF NEGOTIATIONS

The present structure of national (industrial) negotiations came into existence with the formation of permanent national associations of employers. It may be crudely divided into three different types of machinery. Most important in setting the climate of British industrial relations is the structure covering some 9 million employees and in particular that covering 3 million employees in general engineering.

The only permanent rules to be regarded as formally binding on the parties in these industries are the "procedures for the settlement of differences" or the individual employee grievance procedure. The purpose of these procedures is to remove a dispute out of the plant situation once the parties have registered a failure to agree, to pass it upwards through a district or regional conference and, if necessary, finally to a national conference. The procedure by which a grievance is taken up almost always begins with a complaint to a supervisor after which the shop steward may approach first the supervisor, then higher levels of management. If a settlement is not concluded within the plant, it passes outside of the establishment (and outside of the company) to a district conference which involves a full-time official of the union as well as representatives of the employer's association. (Usually these are management of other companies since the number of professionals employed by both sides is minute compared with the U.S. and northern Europe.) The nature of the works, district, and national conferences varies immensely. The engineering industry's procedure is the most influential, however, since it covers most of the British-owned automobile and aerospace industries. Established after two long and successful lockouts in 1898 and 1922, it emphasizes not only the employer's "right to manage" but also the employer association's right to adjudicate at both district and national levels on complaints made by employees against their members.

In terms of mere coverage, another system, that of the Joint Industrial Committees (JICs) or "Whitley Committees," is probably more important. Like the former procedural agreements JICs arose out of the experiences of the early twentieth century. However, they differ insofar as they are the direct result of a government initiative in 1916 when they appointed a committee under the chairmanship of Mr. J. H. Whitley (Deputy Speaker in the House of Commons) to make recommendations "for securing a permanent improvement in the relations between employers and workmen." This committee concluded that an essential condition for securing such an improvement was "adequate organisation on the part of both employers and work people." As a result of this and other government urging, there was general movement in British industry to set up collective bargaining machinery in 1919. In the postwar slump which immediately followed and its aftermath most of the early JICs collapsed. It is doubtful whether this early initiative could have survived without the example of the government in continuing to use collective bargaining based on the Whitley model as a means to settle the terms and conditions of employment within the public services.

At present there are over 200 JICs in operation. They are composed of equal numbers of employer and employee representatives, appointed by their respective associations. Joint secretaries are appointed with the chairman's position alternating annually between the parties. A National JIC is responsible for preparing and operating the constitution, aims, and objects of the council. They are responsible for negotiating the national wages and conditions agreement and for drafting and maintaining a grievance procedure. This procedure may, and often does, contain machinery for conciliation and arbitration apart from that provided on a universal basis by state bodies. The number of employees covered by such machinery is probably a little greater than the former procedural arrangements, there being about 3 million employees in private industry and 6.5 million in public services and public corporations covered by such arrangements.

The major difference between these two forms of machinery is that in the engineering model the emphasis has been placed upon dealing with individual grievances, and there is little in the way of permanent "official" liaison between the parties. In the JICs the setting up of standing machinery ensures a regular discussion of a common agenda and a much clearer allocation of rights and responsibilities within the substantive agreement. It does not imply, however, that such agreements are any more binding than those agreed within the "ad hoc" bodies. Until recently, agreements have not been regarded as binding over a fixed period, and any part can usually be renegotiated whenever both sides agree. The time and form of negotiations have normally been regarded as a matter of strategy and tactics rather than matters of right. The emphasis placed upon the settlement of grievances, which once reflected the greatly superior market power of employers at the time when such procedures were laid down, has in recent years enabled unions to use a collectively expressed grievance as the basis for a general claim. The distinction often used in other national systems between a dispute of "rights" and a dispute of "interests" cannot be maintained in such a situation; indeed it is a distinction that is entirely foreign to the British system.

The main sections of substantive agreements are narrow and usually cover only minimum hourly rates of wages, maximum hours of work (at normal rates), overtime rates, piecework percentages and procedures, annual holidays, shift allowances, and the guaranteed minimum weekly wage. The open-ended nature of agreements enables negotiated modifications in agreed conditions to be made, and indeed at local level a whole corpus of "custom and practice" may be regarded as part of any current agreement. It is usual in JICs, especially in the public services, for minor amendments to be constantly drafted by a subcommittee of the national JIC. Such agreements are usually very much more comprehensive than those negotiated by the ad hoc bodies. It has always been contended by the parties to agreements in the industries covered by these latter bodies that the limited scope of the substantive agreement was deliberate. The employer associations maintain that they could not take the responsibility of negotiating more extensive agreements which would have to apply within a wide range of plants and markets. (The withdrawal of many large firms may appear to confirm this contention but in general these withdrawals have been related to the introduction of wage payment and work systems which make obsolescent the "payment by results" or incentives criteria implied in many national agreements.) The unions have always preferred to leave the provision of sick, accident, and superannuation benefits to the state. An explanation for the different approaches exhibited between the two types of collective bargaining institutions may be found in the large coverage of single employers within the more successful JICs, especially those in the public services.

The third form of negotiating machinery is solely concerned with substantive issues and may not be considered as collective bargaining at all but rather as statutory wage fixing procedures under the jurisdiction of the Department of Employment and Productivity. The purpose of the machinery is to provide a means of determining wages and conditions of employment in industries or trades where otherwise there is no adequate procedure for doing so and where such conditions have a tendency to fall below a "reasonable standard." The ministry has powers to bring such a council into effect and to appoint not more than three members to it including the chairman. For the rest the council has to consist of equal numbers of employer and employee representatives selected by the minister in consultation with (and in practice on the advice of) the appropriate associations and unions.

The substantive content of the agreements reached in Wages Council are similar to those of other national bodies, and the arguments produced in the process of negotiation are also similar. However, the lack of organisation on both sides, but more particularly on the union side, makes the position of the chairman an extremely powerful one. Once agreement has been reached, a fourteen day period is allowed for objections from those affected before the minister is able to issue a wage regulation order which is legally binding upon those within the industry or trade.

The state has also sought to bolster the collective bargaining system in other ways. Fair wages resolutions passed by the Houses of Parliament make it illegal for contractors to be employed in central government work at less favourable conditions than those negotiated for the industry or trade. Of more widespread consequence, under section 8 of the Terms and Conditions of Employment Act 1959, all agreements made within a trade or industry at either national or local level by a properly representative body may be made universally applicable within a similar occupational group to that for which the agreement was originally transacted. If an employer refuses to accede to the request of a union for these terms to apply within his establishment, that union may ask the minister (i.e. the regional officer of the Department of Employment) to intervene on their behalf. If the minister is satisfied as to the appropriateness of the claim it can be referred to the Industrial Court. This Court has the power to impose the agreement upon the employer.

This long, drawn out procedure reflects the universal underlying desire among the parties to agreements in British collective bargaining to avoid legal intervention wherever possible. The decisions to take another party to an agreement to court stand out among the few major attempts to modify the slight body of common law which exists.

Nevertheless, there has been growing public concern at the inadequacy of industrial relations institutions in the U.K. The procedures existing within key areas of the economy pertain to a period in which management authority was greater and qualitatively different from that which exists today. In conditions of high and inelastic demand in both the labour and product markets, employers have been inclined to ignore substantive agreements made at national level and to make up locally paid earnings with new and unauthorized "lieu" bonuses and "systematized" overtime working. For similar reasons the bargaining powers of the shop steward have increased and for the most part have not been restricted by any locally agreed procedures.

The existence of such de facto power at the local level combined with the increasing inadequacy of national procedures, both because of their length (often up to nine months is spent in processing a grievance to national level) and by the unrealism of "employer conciliation" (Engineering Industry Procedure for Avoiding Disputes), has created a situation in which formal institutions reflect very little of the reality. Two measures of their present lack of control are the increasing disparity between high local earnings and low basic rates negotiated at national level and the steep rise in the level of unconstitutional strikes (i.e. those in breach of procedure). Concern with the inflationary effect of the "earnings/price spiral" and the economically debilitating effect of "wildcat" strikes led the government to set up a Royal Commission on Trades Unions and Employers Associations in 1965 under the chairmanship of Lord Donovan.

The Report of the Donovan Commission published in 1968 suggested that the movement towards company or plant-based fixed term agreements, which had been discernible among some large firms during the 1960s, should be taken as a model for the collective bargaining structure of the future. Such agreements should be comprehensive in their substantive content and should include "swift and equitable" grievance procedures, wherever possible terminating in local mediation or arbitration. National agreements should do no more than lay down guidelines in a way which could be followed in the advice and aid to be offered by staff experts working with the national negotiators, who would in effect be assessors of the extent to which each local agreement followed their national criteria. As a first move towards the setting up of this system, the government immediately sent out a request to firms to register agreements with the Division of Manpower and Productivity of the Department of Employment and Productivity (DEP).

It is apparent that most of the agreements so far registered fall well short of the Donovan criteria; it is equally certain that the resources and expertise required to put them into effect are not present within either employer associations or trade unions. In order to bring about such a shift in resources, the government would have to provide high incentives to many local employers and union representatives who, in the short run, will see little or no return and possible disadvantage from a more formalized pattern of industrial relations. Alternatively, the law might be used as an architect of change in the manner of the American Taft-Hartley reforms. It is to this latter course that the present Conservative administration returned in June 1970 is committed.

THE LEGAL FRAMEWORK

Since the early nineteenth century the law has adopted an abstentionist role. To be more specific, whenever an injunction, either criminal or civil, has made some inroad into the individual freedoms enjoyed by the parties, statutory law has restored them within a short period. This was so in 1871 when the Trade Union Act which provided a definition for trade unions and employer associations also freed them from legal liability for acts "in restraint of trade." The act created a scheme for the voluntary registration of trade unions or employer associations within which the unions received tax concessions and some administrative advantages in return for allowing some general principles of good management to be applied to their rules and funds by the Registrar of Friendly Societies.

Since that time a number of actions in tort have been filed by employers in attempts to challenge the unions' power to call a strike, and some modifications have been made to the blanket exceptions. Under the 1875 act, no one can be prosecuted for criminal conspiracy in the circumstances of a trade dispute for something which would not in other circumstances be considered criminal *except* if in breaking one's contract of employment one knows that it is likely to endanger human life, cause serious injury, or damage valuable property. This latter condition is made more specific for gas, water, and electricity supply workers who commit a criminal act if their actions result in the loss of supply to the consumer. Both the Merchant Shipping Act 1894 and the Police Acts 1919 and 1964 limited the freedom to strike of seamen and police by forbidding them to disobey orders while performing their duties. During the two World Wars and in the 1927 Trade Disputes and Trade Union Act the right to strike was somewhat diluted. There is little evidence to show that any of these statutory limitations had much effect, and many recent strikes by gas, water, and electricity workers have certainly affected consumer supply without any action being taken against the perpetrators. This was also so during the twelve-month period from August 1966 to August 1967 in which it was a statutory offence to take "any action, and in particular any action by way of taking part, or persuading others to take part, in a strike, with a view to compel or induce any employer to implement an award or settlement in respect of employment" at a time when its implementation was contrary to the incomes freeze then in operation. Offenders were liable to a fine up to £500 on conviction by indictment. Despite violations no one was in fact indicted.

One notorious attempt by an employer to restrict the actions of unions was that of the *Taff Vale Railyway Company* v. *The Amalgamated Society of Railway Servants* in 1901. In this case the House of Lords maintained that the registration of a union had given it semicorporate status thus enabling it to be sued straight-forwardly for damages in respect of torts committed by its agents. In 1906 a newly formed radical Liberal government with the help of a just-formed Labour Party passed an act restoring the immunity of the unions from tort and for any liability for inducing a breach of contract of employment through striking an employer in the course of negotiations with him. However, in the case of *Stratford* v. *Lindley* (1964) trade union officials were found to have procured breaches in *commercial contract*. This position has been supported in subsequent legal judgments, and it appears therefore that the use of the secondary boycott affecting a third party may leave a union official open to damages, though not against the organisation. More generally it has been held that each individual employee who goes on strike without first giving notice of his intention to break his individual contract of employment may be sued by his employer for damages. Needless to say, such cases are rare.

Employer actions against unions have generally been directed at exposing union funds to tort liability. Other actions taken by members of unions have attempted to bring external constraints upon the internal workings of unions. Little control, beyond publication of accounts and the investment of funds, is exercised by the Registrar. In 1910 a member of the same Society of Railway Servants sued his union for misuse of funds in the support of a political party. This resulted in an act in 1913 permitting any objects to be legitimate provided the statutory ones were paramount; however, any member may "contract out" of contributing to the political fund, and an aggrieved contributor may appeal to the Registrar.

Two recent cases have also concerned the control of the union over its members. These have dealt with the ability of the union to prevent lapsed members from continuing their employment in "union shops" or finding employment in "closed shops." In the first case (*O'Leary* v. *NUVB* February 1970) it was held that union rules are subject to the rules of "natural justice." The second case (*Edwards* v. *SOGAT* August 1970) held that the "right to work" cannot be taken away by a union without public scrutiny. This latter is obviously a fundamental modification of the freedom of the union to impose its authority upon individuals for the purposes of gaining bargaining strength. Together with the restraints imposed on the use of the secondary boycott, the two cases mark a substantial movement towards curbing the official strength of the unions.

This is particularly important in Britain because the rights and obligations which underlie a collective bargaining system, which in most other countries are defined and upheld in a statutory labour code, are in the British context maintained by the ability of each party to exert private sanctions against the other. Thus the act of joining or organising a union is under the 1871 act not an illegal act, but if an employee loses his job for doing either he generally has no recourse to law. "Yellow dog" contracts are nevertheless unusual. One of the most extensive forms of this type of contract was practiced by the Engineering Employers Association, which sponsored a Foremen and Staff Mutual Benefit Society, membership in which required that an employee would lose all the pensions and insurance benefits obtained through the society if his employers discovered that he was a union member. This clause in the Society's constitution was made illegal by act of Parliament in 1969 after a successful union campaign against it.

British law also has had little to say on the recognition of trade unions for bargaining purposes. The boards of most nationalised industries are required by the statutes under which they were created to set up negotiating machinery, although the meaning of these requirements has never been tested at law. In general there is no legal obligation on employers to recognise unions or to bargain with them. In the case of manual workers, cases are increasingly confined to small employers, though some very large American employers such as Kodak and IBM have successfully resisted unionisation. In tight labour markets and in the light of the provisions of section 8 of the Terms and Conditions of Employment Act it is increasingly difficult for them to hold out against recognition. The formal existence of a grievance procedure only, however, enables limited recognition for the purposes of processing individual grievances to be used as a successful ploy by members of employer associations. Acceptance of unions as bargaining agents for nonmanual employees is still unusual. This is a major obstacle to unionisation in these growing sectors of employment where prior recognition is perceived as a precondition for membership by more conformist and more career-oriented employees.

The obligation to maintain a collective agreement is also generally regarded to be not sustainable at law. Certainly this was the intention of section 4 (i) of the 1871 act, and this view was sustained in a recent case, *Ford Motor Co.* v. *The Transport and General Workers Union and Amalgamated Union of Engineers and Foundry Workers*. On the other hand, a few agreements have recently been signed which imply an acceptance of legal obligation on the part of the signatories. If these are to be tested, it must first be established that the signatories of agreements are the agents of their respective associations. This appears to be a somewhat obscure point in spite of the Ministry of Labour opinion (Guidance to the Royal Commission 1965, p. 83) that the *Taff Vale* ruling was still applicable in this circumstance to unregistered unions.

During the parliamentary election of June 1970 the Conservatives proposed that collective agreements should be on a par with other forms of contract and should be legally enforceable against the employing company or the union whose representatives signed the agreement, unless it was stated otherwise in the agreement. Breaches of contract would be heard in a newly constituted branch of the High Court with regional divisions each having a legally trained chairman and equal numbers of lay members selected from nominees from the two sides of industry. Strikes to enforce a closed or union shop, interunion disputes, sympathetic strikes or lockouts, and strikes to prevent management taking on certain types of labour would be illegal. In strikes or lockouts involving the national interest it would be possible for the minister to apply to this new form of Industrial Court for an injunction imposing a "cooling-off" period of up to 80 days during which time a Board of Inquiry could arrange a ballot on the strike.

These proposals are of course similar to much existing American procedure. This similarity extends to the legal duty imposed by their proposals on employers to recognise and negotiate with registered unions subject to a majority of their employees desiring recognition. A ballot might be taken by a DEP official, and if the employer failed to honour the result the union could file a complaint to the Industrial Court, which could make a binding award. Registration of unions would, however, be made compulsory, and the Registrar would have a duty to ensure that union rules are democratic and not contrary to the public interest. Pre-entry closed shops would be illegal and the imposition of union shops severely restricted.

17

CONCILIATION, ARBITRATION, AND COMMITTEES OF INQUIRY

Some of the JIC procedures have their own arrangements for arbitration or conciliation, but these are largely confined to the public services. Private industry relies almost exclusively on the provisions made by the state in these respects. Most of the minister's legal powers of conciliation, arbitration, and inquiry derive from the Conciliation Act 1896 and the Industrial Courts Act 1919. The latter act stemmed, as does so much of the present formal structure of collective bargaining, from the Whitley Committee Report. The boards in the public services such as the Civil Service Arbitration Tribunal are set up according to the provisions of the Industrial Courts Act.

Since World War I, the Department of Employment has provided a Conciliation Service staffed by officials in every region. These may be approached by one of the parties to the dispute, or the conciliator may, according to statute, invite the parties to meet under his chairmanship. They may of course refuse, but if they meet and reach a conclusion the responsibility for it is the parties', the state having no further responsibility. The number of differences at which conciliation takes place is only a small proportion (about 13 percent) of the annual number of stoppages. However, a growing number of national stoppages are involving the mediating services of the chief conciliator, the minister himself, and even the Prime Minister.

The minister may if he thinks fit and with the consent of both parties refer an existing or contemplated dispute for arbitration to an Industrial Court, to a single arbitrator appointed by him, or to a board consisting of an equal number of employer and employee representatives under an independent chairman nominated by the minister. The Court is a permanent body whereas the board may be selected directly by the respective bodies. Single arbitrators are appointed by the minister; they usually operate in a more flexible manner than boards or courts. It is usual practice not to publish the findings of the single arbitrators nor those of boards unless the parties wish it. In any case British arbitrators do not discuss the merits of the rival cases when announcing their awards. There is therefore little in their statement which offers a guide to those who have to put their award into effect or to those who might build a body of common law from their decisions. Of these procedures the Industrial Court is the one most used.

The trend in arbitration had been upwards in all cases until the late 1960s, when such procedures came into some disapprobation. Arbitration, however, has been much less favoured than conciliation, there being some 57 arbitration cases in the average year during 1960-65 as against roughly 350 conciliations. Both are used in only a small proportion of the cases, and the requirement for both parties to agree to arbitration has almost certainly reduced the chances of such procedures being used as compared to the more interventionary powers of the conciliation officer.

In the two World Wars compulsory arbitration has replaced the right to strike in certain cases. Under the provisions of the Conditions of Employment and National Arbitration Order (S.R.O. 1305) the minister gained wide powers of compulsion in the labour market including the ability to prohibit strikes or lockouts in any disputes for a three-week period, during which he could refer the matter to local arbitration tribunals whose decision was legally binding on the parties. This power was extended until 1951 when it was replaced by the Industrial Disputes Order setting up a new form of local tribunal. After that time arbitration was compulsory only in the sense that either party could take a dispute to the minister for reference to the Tribunal without the consent of the other party and that any award of this body was legally binding upon both parties. This order was replaced in 1959 by the already described, much diluted provisions of the Terms and Conditions of Employment Act. In acquiescing in that act the unions traded arbitration away in return for greater employment security. Since that time, however, many trade unions have expressed a desire to return to the former system of unilateral arbitration. There is plentiful evidence for the view that the ability to impose an arbitration award on employers had assisted unions, particularly white-collar unions, in obtaining their subsequent recognition.

A politically important power given by the Conciliation Act

and Industrial Courts Act is that of public inquiry. For this purpose the minister can appoint Courts of Inquiry and Committees of Investigation. A third form of inquiry is that in which the brief goes beyond the circumstances of the dispute with terms of reference extending to an examination of the long-term labour problems within an industry. These represent an extension of ministerial powers in recent years which go beyond those given by the acts.

The Court of Inquiry is regarded as a last resort. It is not an instrument of conciliation or arbitration and it does no more than make recommendations upon which a reasonable settlement can be based. It usually consists of three members appointed by the minister: it takes evidence on oath and generally in public. Its findings are laid before Parliament and may be discussed there. The findings of individual (or Committee) arbitrators are not treated in this formal way.

Such Courts and Committees are infrequent, about two or three of each taking place in a typical year. In the past they have been regarded as an important means of exposing a situation and in breaking an impasse and thus allowing the parties to review their bargaining position from a fresh standpoint. In recent years the growing government concern over matters of industrial efficiency and organisation have led to an increasing use of the Committee of Inquiry under the minister's general powers. On the basis of such a one on labour problems in the port transport industry in 1964 (Lord Devlin), a wide ranging fundamental reorganisation of the industry was undertaken.

This growing governmental desire for public inquiry, rather than for conciliation and compromise, reached its apotheosis in the setting up of the National Board for Prices and Incomes (NBPI) in April 1965. This is (at the time of writing) a permanent body of 15 members appointed by the minister with a secretariat and research staff numbering some 300. It forms a separate department from the ministry but it is ultimately responsible to the minister. Since 1965 the NBPI has been a major means of investigating issues, not with a view to settling a dispute but in order to set the aims of the parties against the criteria of government incomes policy. In 1968 the name of the government ministry responsible for labour was changed to the Department of Employment and Productivity (DEP) denoting a distinct shift from its former conciliatory role to one of active interventionism. This interventionism was primarily inspired by the belief that industrial relations problems were a symptom of a much more fundamental malaise. A Division of Manpower and Productivity (DMP) was set up within the DEP which extended the regional conciliation service offered by the Department to one of problem diagnosis and consultancy by newly recruited experts in management systems and company organisation as well as industrial relations. These services might be offered on the initiative of a conciliator or requested by management involved in a dispute. However, in 1968 the DMP were given the task of registering all existing collective agreements, a task which carried with it the opportunity to offer the Department's services in respect to any inadequacies perceived to be present. In all of these tasks such state agencies have negligible powers of compulsion and must rely on their ability to persuade or to morally coerce the parties into agreeing to their presence in the situation and later to their proposed remedies.

This type of persuasive interventionism was seen by the Royal Commission as being the principle means to procedural changes as well as to the more substantive issues which were the concern of the NBPI. As a direct result of the Donovan proposals the Labour government set up a Commission for Industrial Relations in March 1969 whose functions were to investigate cases in which employers have refused to recognise a union having been requested to do so; to encourage reforms in trade union structure and services; to investigate cases where there is a failure to negotiate satisfactory agreements; and to be particularly concerned with the effectiveness of existing procedures. This Commission has been set up by order in council (i.e. it has so far not gained statutory status) consisting of six permanent commissioners and about one hundred secretarial and research staff. The Commission was seen by the Royal Commission Report as one of the major architects of change in bringing about the movement to formal local agreements and the extension of collective bargaining to nonunionised firms. Its status is similar to that of the NBPI and its work is received through a ministerial reference; such a reference was, according to Donovan, to be chosen on the basis that it provided an important guide to other parties in similar situations.

Because of the purely voluntary nature of the exercise, its investigators have therefore relied heavily on the fact that the minister has consulted both the CBI and the TUC before referring a case to the commission for Industrial Relations. This procedure has resulted in a slow start to the Commission's work. It has so far investigated only seven recognition disputes in its first fifteen months. In five cases they have met with some success in persuading employers to recognise unions. Ballots have not been used since "a ballot does not take place in a vacuum but against a background of known management policy and attitudes which can strongly affect the outcome. . . . An attitude survey can give some of the results to be expected from a ballot, but in addition can cover a much wider range of information."[4]

The question to be asked is whether faced with an intensely suspicious trade union movement (in spite of the fact that the Commission's chairman is a former general secretary of the TUC) and a cool CBI the Commission can produce results of sufficient significance to transform the present fragmented and socially costly system merely through example and persuasion. It is clear that more "progressive" unions and management have been influenced to improve relatively trouble-free procedures, but it is doubtful whether many small employers can be affected by example. A "note of reservation" made by a member of the Royal Commission to its Report suggested powers to compel parties to accept CIR findings as to jurisdictional disputes, bargaining in good faith, and restrictive practices. It now seems likely that these legal powers may be included in the Conservative programme of legislation.

It is difficult to pronounce upon the future of either arbitration

4. Commission on Industrial Relations, *Report No. 9, First General Report,* HMSO, Cmnd. 4417.

or conciliation under the new administration. The minister is clearly planning to revert to the traditional forms of conciliation wherever possible and may withdraw from substantive intervention as it relates to incomes policy and with its concern for managerial efficiency; probably greater emphasis will be given to procedural enforcement. However, the Conservative election platform included both the legally enforceable collective contract and statutory constraints on labour "restrictive practices." The first may well drive the arbitration process downwards to be incorporated in the plant or company agreement. The latter form of investigation may require the resurrection of a national body with the familiar form of the National Board for Prices and Incomes.

THE ECONOMIC ENVIRONMENT

After taking into account interindustry differences the level of unionisation has been highly correlated with the general level of economic activity in Britain. Yet it would be wrong to see the extent of formal union membership as reflecting an increase in union bargaining power in any straightforward manner. This is because at such times the internal authority of union leaders has tended to be eroded by the increased de facto power of the union lay officials on the shop floor. Unlike unions in many other countries the core of full-time paid officials in British organisations is relatively small, and most of the work in the recruitment and servicing of new members rests with elected representatives. The formal structure of the unions has been slow to adapt to the movement in power brought by full employment. Much greater stress has continued to be placed on the centralised formal channels of authority and communication. In this way the unions see themselves as being better able to cope with recessions in economic activity in which their members would become dependent upon their combined strength of numbers.

There were also other fairly obvious needs for central cohesion, but these were ignored in the failure of union leaders formally to recognise and integrate the role and increased status of their local lay representatives within the machinery of the unions. These officials whose formal role usually amounted to no more than the collection of dues became the chief spokesmen and negotiators within bargaining units throughout industry, particularly in the automobile industry. It is these shop stewards rather than central union leaders who have structured and, as a result of their uncoordinated actions, determined union actions during periods of high economic activity.

Much of the momentum to take advantage of the scarcity of labour has, then, been generated on the shop floor rather than in nationally agreed policies; but any autonomous move to capitalise on temporary labour shortages has had secondary effects which have far exceeded the initial upwards push given to wage rates within a single establishment or local labour market. A number of recent studies have shown most wage claims to relate to wage structures or to differentials in remuneration. In other words an initial desire on the part of a group of workers within a plant or industry to improve their position vis-a-vis other groups has led to a chain reaction of claims from other groups who wish to restore their position relative to the first or to one of the many groups who responded to the initial rise.

As a result of this largely uncontrolled "whip-sawing" effect of local bargaining it has become extremely difficult for unions or for employer associations to formulate realistic negotiating strategies at national level. The insufficiencies of the system are such that neither side has the resources to devote to recording information on such a scale. Without either de facto power to control local bargaining or knowledge of what is happening, the extent of the membership of unions and employer associations in much of private industry is a somewhat misleading guide to the actual ability of these organisations to determine policy.

This is perhaps best illustrated by an examination of the widening range of incomes among manual workers. Even among Health Service manual employees, one of the lowest paid groups in the country, earnings range from £13.6 a week to £26.4 a week, and in other areas such as docks, automobiles, and printing, where incentive and piecework schemes have in the recent past been widely used, the difference in earnings can commonly amount to a factor of 6 to 8. At the top end of this range the earnings of many manual workers exceed those of white-collar workers including civil servants, nurses, etc. As a result of this and other factors many white-collar workers are themselves anxious to join a union with a similarly locally aggressive policy or to change the character of their professional association.

From the government standpoint the autonomous nature of this secondary drift in earnings has serious inflationary consequences which in turn affect the ability of industry to remain price competitive in world product markets. It has been the goal of successive administrations since 1961 to impose some form of constraint on incomes. Between 1947 and 1950 the trade unions cooperated with the Labour Chancellor of the Exchequer in constraining wage claims. By 1961 the nature of the problem was much better appreciated (the OECD Report "The Problem of Rising Prices" had considerable impact on government opinion); the then Conservative chancellor tackled it by means of a "pay pause" in which the public services were both to act as examples and to hold down secondary drift. This lasted only six months, during which time the government refused to recognise public service arbitration awards and the chancellor enjoined arbitrators to take the "public interest" into account in making future awards.

Over the next few years much more emphasis was placed on increasing productivity through capital expansion. Trade unions and employers co-operated in the preparation of a prognostic document entitled "Conditions Necessary for Faster Growth" published by the National Economic Development Council in 1963. In the following year the newly elected Labour Prime Minister formed a Department of Economic Affairs which was to be responsible for indicative planning over a seven-year period. In a declaration of intent employers and unions pledged their support for a "planned growth in incomes"—planned, that is, in relation to increases in productivity. In a White Paper "Prices and Incomes Policy" (Cmnd. 2639, April 1965) the government confirmed its intention that increases in earnings should not generally rise above a norm of 3 to 3.5 percent per annum and that exceptions to the norm could only be justified in terms of six criteria, one being that of the abnormally low level of the supplicants' present remuneration. The most important criterion was, however, the ability to show a substantial gain in productivity directly attributable to changes in labour practices. The initial plan involved the CBI representatives on one side and the TUC on the other. Its short-term effect on plant managers and shop floor workers appears to have been minimal. Earnings continued to increase at a faster rate than output and capital investment did not move appreciably upwards.

The crisis appeared, as it usually does, in the external money market in July 1966. Faced with dwindling gold and currency reserves the government rapidly changed its economic strategy. Instead of the voluntary acceptance of the incomes norm, a statutory freeze was imposed until June 1967, subject to exceptions which became a little less restricted in the second half of the period. The government retained power to defer a proposed pay or price increase for up to seven months subject to reference to the National Board for Prices and Incomes (NBPI). In April 1968 the government spelled out the initial criteria for exceptions in greater detail and announced an increased emphasis on prices. In July of that year the Prices and Incomes Act 1968 gave the government power, subject to recommendation of the Board, to hold up all increases for up to twelve months in all. In December 1969 an incomes norm of 2.5 to 4 percent was announced for 1970. The method of voluntary notification used throughout most of this period was to continue, but powers to delay implementation of proposed increases which appeared to infringe the incomes policy for a period of up to three months were retained subject, once more, to a reference being made to the Board.

The most important changes in the labour market brought about by this policy were probably not related to its restraining effects on either earnings or prices. Over the whole period the rate of increase in money earnings was greater than the rate of increase in output per head and of prices, the rate of increase in prices in 1968/69 being almost twice the average over the previous decade. In this last year, however, productivity (output per head) was almost 4 percent higher than the average for the previous decade. Unlike all other recorded increases in productivity it was achieved during a period of monetary and credit restriction, with unemployment at its highest postwar level. Though some of the credit for this may be due to the nature of the unemployment, some of which was created by a poll tax on employers of clerical and service workers, much must also have been due to the negotiation of 3,500 productivity agreements involving over 6 million workers. The productivity "gate" through the incomes "norm" allowed many dubious locally and nationally negotiated deals to pass: all agreements had to be registered with the DEP and only a few were investigated by the DMP or NBPI. However, the latter body was responsible for setting a new climate of negotiating in which for the most calculative reasons most large unions became more interested in work measurement and manpower planning.

The National Board for Prices and Income's work arose directly out of references from the minister (the Secretary of State for Employment and Productivity). Under the Prices and Incomes legislation wage claims and proposals to increase wages and prices were to be reported to the minister, who might then (within 30 days) refer them to the Board. In practice such references were usually made after consultation with the CBI and TUC; the minister relied heavily upon these bodies for prior information on proposed increases despite the statutory liability for a fine of up to £50 on those failing to notify the DEP of such increases. The Board had wide powers of investigation and might require "such estimates, returns or other information as may be specified or described in the summons" (Prices and Incomes Act 1966). Its method of study and report was (and still is today) essentially that of the empirical case study carried out by social scientists or by industrial relations practitioners. There was never any attempt to take evidence in the form of a judicial hearing either privately or publicly.

Its reports and recommendations are presented to Parliament and published generally.

The major function of the Board over this period was to pronounce upon whether claims for wages or price increases should be allowed under the exceptions to the national norm. In fact the chairman interpreted his brief in the widest possible sense and published far-ranging critiques of the structure of any industry or plant under scrutiny and of its industrial relations. In two reports, for example, it was suggested that the range of earnings in Wage Council industries was such as to make nonsense of the statutory minima imposed upon them, and that the educative function of the councils seemed also to be largely not working. More recently references have included general problems such as the causes of low pay in some sectors, including manual workers in the public services.

Even the little use made of arbitration has declined since 1966. To some extent the NBPI has acted as an alternative to arbitration similar to a Committee of Inquiry. Some claims which clearly might have gone to arbitration eventually have been analysed and pronounced upon by the Board in such a way that both parties have been forced to re-examine their cases. On the other hand, where an arbitration award might not have appeared acceptable to the parties the Board has been available as an investigatory body. An extension of its role has been that of a standing review body on the pay and salaries of the armed services and (up to May 1970) of university teachers. At the same time under incomes legislation it has examined awards made by other standing committees, that for the higher civil service and that for medical practitioners.

Almost certainly the Conservative government will end or modify the functions of the Board. About 40 percent of British employees have been affected by its pronouncements. Its work has been resented by labour because references of wage demands has implied a delay which on average has lasted nearly six months. (At one stage the minister was referring nearly all notified claims to the Board simply in order to delay payment.) Management have resented the Board's suggestions that low productivity has resulted from inefficient control and utilisation of labour and from disorderly wage structures.

Its effect on recent awards made by arbitrators and Wages Councils appears to be minimal insofar as evidence has continued to be accepted and adjudged in the traditional manner. However, the existence of the "public interest" as represented in the incomes policy "norm" has been in the background of these awards. This has created a crisis of confidence in all such independent rulings, a crisis which has weakened the commitment of parties to the existing machinery in the public services.

During the period of the earnings freeze there was no significant rise in the number of strikes. Yet in 1968 there followed a sharp increase in strike activity and in 1969 the level was the highest ever recorded in the U.K. during this century. There was also a return to the union sanctioned strike: all of the major strikes were union led and a number of public service unions made provision for a strike fund in anticipation of the strategic use of the strike. To some extent this reflected a desire on the part of leadership to maintain or regain control of their members' actions. The leadership of many large unions operating in both private and public sectors changed in the late 1960s, and this may have exacerbated the leaders' desires to establish their authority. Yet underlying this leadership need was a new uncertainty among their members about the operation of negotiating procedures even in JICs and Whitley Council sectors. At the same time most large unions, especially white-collar organisations, have recorded an unprecedented growth over 1969/70.

Neither the existence of the highest postwar level of unemployment nor statutory incomes restrictions have prevented the level of money earnings from rising. The level of expectations appears to have become inured to the high level of unemployment. It is possible that the restrictions on strike activity had some effect during 1966/67; it appears more likely that a flood of frustration and impatience at "unfair" erosions of differentials and lost comparisons has broken loose in a delayed response to political restraints. These frustrations may well have been made worse by the large amount of comparative data released by the NBPI, which has created a more "perfect" market situation in which earnings comparisons are more easily made and action taken to bring net advantages into their former equilibrium.

THE POLITICAL FRAMEWORK

Attempts by government to mediate in industrial disputes go back to 1867. Since the establishment of a government Board of Labour in 1894, conciliation and mediation has been an important role of a state agency. Added to this was the administration of the Factory Acts and other statutes laying down minimum standards of health, welfare and safety, and, in administrative and economic terms, the most important function of running employment exchanges. All of these were essentially supportive activities designed to make a free enterprise system work more effectively. The recent crisis of confidence in existing institutions reflects the growth of interventionism on the part of the state on behalf of the public interest. That this crisis should come to a head under a Socialist government is hardly surprising, that that government relied on the trade union movement for the bulk of its electoral support and finance is obviously something of a paradox.

Since its foundation in 1900 the Labour Party has relied on contributions from the political funds of individual trade unions (not the TUC) to its national funds and to the constituency expenses of about a third of the parliamentary party members who are sponsored by these unions. On the basis of their affiliation, trade union bloc votes dominate annual party conventions, and on occasion they have successfully pressed political resolutions which were contrary to those of the parliamentary party and, even when Labour was in government, contrary to Cabinet policy. The formal power of unions is apparently immense, yet Labour administrations have pursued restrictionist economic policies and hampered the unions' actions on a number of occasions. Indeed, with the exception of the 1927 act, Conservative ministers have been responsible for much more supportive legislation on the statute book than has Labour.

In a sense the conflict is contained within the nature of British unionism. The ideology expressed in the constitution of the TUC and of most large manual unions is articulated in a demand for the public ownership of the means of production and distribution. In practice this amounts to a desire to be consulted on the long-term policies of the government towards industry, while retaining as much freedom as possible to pursue other and separate goals if they see their members' interests as lying elsewhere. Since their concern for the short-term goals of their members is the measure by which trade union officials are judged in the process of internal democracy, they are constantly making compromises with the requirements of the Labour Party leadership and their formal ideology. The nature of the compromises have since the formation of the TUC in 1868 almost always tended to reflect their desire to retain their autonomy and freedom from external constraints or responsibilities. The parliamentary party for its part has since the days of Ramsay MacDonald emphasised that its duty is to the electorate; Labour Members of Parliament have never been afraid to hint at "breach of parliamentary privilege," i.e. undue pressure, if threatened by unions. This has rarely been necessary for, outside of the activities of the TUC, few unions in the private sector have any permanent provision for effective lobbying or even for regular contact and communication with the M.P.s they finance.

THE DEVELOPING ROLE OF THE TUC AND CBI

When the Conservatives were returned in 1951 the general secretary of the TUC announced that it was the intention of the General Council to continue to offer the new government the same cooperation in the making and carrying out of economic policies that it had given to Labour. Both the employer organisations and the TUC had previously been involved in the National Joint Advisory Council during the war and in

31

a similar body under Labour. But during the second postwar Labour government both have been involved in an exercise that began with a Joint Statement of Intent and quickly became a series of defensive strategems designed to ward off government constraints upon their members' actions. Paradoxically, in doing so they have both gained considerably more power over their affiliates than before the government intervened. This is much truer of the TUC than of the CBI. In reply to prices and incomes legislation the TUC set up its own "wage-vetting" machinery to which affiliated members gave notice of proposed wage claims: the CBI set up similar machinery for price increases. Both proved abortive in their initial intention of fending off government compulsion, but the TUC machinery has remained in being, and in 1969 the TUC suggested that they might use it to isolate key bargains within "wage contours." Earlier in 1967 the General Council called the first Conference of the Executive Committees of affiliated unions to be held since 1949. Now it is an annual event held to discuss and endorse a National Economic Review which in the words of the then general secretary "is of the nature of a plan . . . which we believe . . . can help this country to achieve a situation that we have always wanted—of full employment, of rising standards of living, of expanding social services, with reasonable stability at the same time."[5] Clearly these aims are somewhat more pragmatic than those in the TUC constitution.

Apart from this wider function the TUC has since 1921 been concerned with the structure of the movement. In practical terms its only real achievements had been in setting up the so-called Bridlington machinery to prevent and solve interunion disputes over membership. This included provision for joint agreements on spheres of influence and the mutual recognition of cards and transfer of membership. In event of jurisdictional disputes arising, the appellant union has first to raise the matter with the offending union, then, after various stages of TUC mediation have been attempted, the matter may be brought before the TUC Disputes Committee where an award can be

5. TUC, *Economic Review and Report of a Conference of Executive Committees of Affiliated Organisations,* March 1968.

made. Ultimately the only sanction of the TUC is expulsion, but the machinery has had a high degree of success where it has been used. The Royal Commission criticised the machinery on the grounds that the TUC had to wait to be invited before it could intervene in a dispute and therefore many important jurisdictional issues over which strikes occurred were never taken to the TUC. To this adjunction was added the proposal that the Commission on Industrial Relations might become an investigatory body and make recommendations upon such issues. Faced with these external pressures for reform, the affiliated unions gave the General Council power to intervene in inter-union disputes, a power which the general secretary has used in mediating in demarcation, i.e. job assignment, as well as jurisdictional disputes between members.

Similar actions have been initiated in response to the Donovan concern with union rule books, and with the need for an external appeals tribunal in the case of internal actions of unions against individual members. More positively, the TUC has also initiated industrial conferences on the future collective bargaining strategy to be adopted within each industry. The form of the TUC's present actions is generally tentative, and it is difficult to know how far it can be taken in the face of the strength of the three large general unions. Nevertheless it is important to note that the executive committees of several large white-collar associations catering to professional employees have recommended their members to affiliate their organisations with the TUC over the past twelve months. Experience has shown that the effects of such bodies upon the influence and workings of the TUC go far beyond their relative numerical strength. On the other hand, the effect of affiliation has, if anything, made these new affiliates more favourable towards militant action in support of their own bargaining goals and more inclined to express radical political opinions.

·II·

Negotiation in
Public Employment and the
Civil Service

IN the British context the meaning of public employment extends far beyond those employees whose remuneration comes either directly or indirectly out of taxation by local or national government. Only three areas of public service unionisation are covered within this volume, these three being the major areas in which central negotiations are conducted with representatives of national government in respect to awards paid out of central taxation. A fourth, that of education, in which agreements are funded from both central and local taxation, together with services administered and largely paid for by local authorities (city government) are the subject of a separate text.

Each of these examples provides interesting case studies in themselves, but in order to understand the importance of the government influence on industrial relations it is useful to consider that total public expenditure (excluding national debt interest) has increased as a proportion of gross national product from 13 percent in 1910 to well over 40 percent during the middle 1960s. Of the working population of nearly 24 million, nearly 7 million are in some form of public employment. Over 3.5 million of this total is paid out of direct taxation, a total which was even greater until the change of status in the Post Office in October 1969 reduced the number of civil servants by nearly 450,000.

The influence of the government as an employer is therefore immense. First, as a "good employer" it sets an example in respect to its behaviour towards over a quarter of the working population in its employ. Second, it has a duty to manage the economy, which implies that in any advice or policy decision which it imposes on outside employers and unions it will behave in a similar fashion within its own field of employment, or even set an example. In the first role the government has certainly tried to set an example in recognising and negotiating with unions since the early part of the century but most especially since 1919. Before this date the Fair Wages Resolution of 1910 had already gone some way to ensure that the state did not employ labour at less than the going rate of earnings within the trade or industry.

In the series of acts by which the major utilities were brought under public control from 1946 until 1948 and more recently in the Iron and Steel Corporation Act 1967 and Post Office Corporation Act 1969, the minister was required to consult with any organisation that appeared to be representative of employees. The most specific of the statutory requirements was that such machinery as was established should be not less favourable than that which had previously existed. Some later legislation became more specific. Section 7 of the Atomic Energy Authority Act 1954 charged the new Authority with the duty of concluding agreements with "appropriate" organisations, for the establishment of machinery for the negotiation of terms and conditions of empolyment including reference to arbitration in cases of failures to agree, and for consultation on matters of safety, health, welfare, and any other matters of mutual interest to employees and management. The Iron and Steel Act went further and legislated for the appointment of at least one director to the national and each of the regional boards of directors, selected from among shop-floor workers by the minister, who was to be advised in his selection by the trade unions.

While this latter is to be regarded as experimental, it reflects the efforts made by government to ensure that in all public establishments the Whitley recommendations of 1917 are carried through in the spirit in which they were made, that is, "What is wanted is that work people should have a greater opportunity of participating in the discussion about and adjustment of those parts of industry by which they are most affected." The recognition of unions and this kind of employer commitment have given a very real impetus to trade unionism in the public services. This is especially so in the white-collar areas of public employment. Comparisons made within this text will demonstrate that the usual relationship between the level of unionisation and the manual-nonmanual occupational dichotomy with respect to union membership is reversed in the public services. In most sectors of the nonindustrial civil service, for example, 90 percent or more of the white-collar staff are in unions, while in many government industrial establishments union membership may be as low as 30 percent. This state of affairs demonstrates the ability of white-collar employees to take advantage of bargaining machinery when encouraged to do so. Given their greater career commitment and security of employment, salaried workers have tended to take much fuller advantage of the statutory duty to consult with employees which was laid upon public employers than have the weekly wage-paid staff. They have also normally been aided by the existence of occupationally based unions within which to develop their special negotiating interests, as opposed to the more general and widely based unions organising manual workers.

NEGOTIATING MACHINERY AND PROBLEMS IN THE LOCATION OF EMPLOYER AUTHORITY

The structure of collective bargaining that has been almost universally adopted in the public services has been that of the Joint Industrial Council or Whitley machinery. This is a permanent and, usually, three-tiered structure of committees or councils set up to determine the levels of wages and working conditions of employees within the industry. Normally the National Council sets national rates and conditions designed to apply throughout the sector of public employment that it covers. Intermediate machinery within the industry at departmental and/or regional level has a duty to apply these national rules and to add or to modify them in relation to the circumstances that exist in the area of their jurisdiction. Generally the powers of the councils at this level are circumscribed by the need to refer all major modifications that change the general applicability of the terms negotiated at national level to the superior body for approval. In this way the national agreements are policed by the JIC machinery at each level, and predictability and central control is thus ensured.

Possibly as important as this higher level machinery is the local council or works committee which underlies the Whitley structure. These councils were seen to be the basis upon which the co-operation of employees was to be secured in the attainment of the goals of the whole organisation. At the same time they ensure that the grievances of employees are not allowed to fester but are dealt with swiftly and in the right atmosphere with a degree of understanding that can only be achieved at local level. In fact a number of public services have carried with them an attachment to a national grievance procedure under private ownership, and other sectors of public employment such as the National Health Service have established an individual appeals procedure subsequent to the setting up of what proved to be inadequate Whitley procedures.

These councils are established with wide briefs to discuss all matters concerning the well-being of the industry and its employees. The vagueness of this definition is deliberate and has allowed the development of an attitude towards negotiations in some sectors of public employment which discounts conflict and places an emphasis on a common problem-solving approach. Nevertheless, the distinction between bargaining and consultation has been maintained by the dichotomy between agenda items which may be referred to arbitration·in event of failure to agree and those on which management will prevail. Normally the arbitrable subjects are confined to matters of pay, hours, and holidays. This has been so even in the most successful of Whitley contexts, i.e. the civil service.

Most JIC agreements have compulsory arbitration arrangements built into the bargaining structure. (One, the Burnham Committee structure for teachers in primary and secondary education, has a statutorily enforced arbitration procedure.) For this purpose special panels of arbitrators have been set up by most JICs, one nominated by management, the other by the staff side. All appointments to such special arbitration tribunals, including the appointment of a neutral chairman, are made by the minister responsible for reporting on behalf of the industry to Parliament.

The formal powers of the minister in respect to all public employees are usually very wide whether in concerns that are operated according to commercial criteria, such as nationalised industries or public corporations, or in direct government employment. In practice the executive control of public concerns rests at a somewhat lower level. In public corporations it is exercised by boards of directors appointed by the minister but ultimately responsible to him (see Chapter IV, the Post Office). In central government the Treasury has exercised direct control over the administration of the civil service for most of this century. In 1969, however, this control passed into the hands of a newly created executive department responsible to separate ministers in Parliament. Yet despite the large numbers of public employees and vast public expenditure on services and works, the proportion of the working population directly employed by the government is very much less than in any other European country.

The reason for this is the dispersion of both responsibility and financial authority across public corporations and local city government. Staff employed by these latter governments, or local authorities, make up nearly 300,000 more than centrally employed civil servants. The local authorities themselves contribute at least 50 percent of the finance for such staff out of locally collected taxes but make up the whole of the employer's side of the National Joint Councils. In public corporations executive board appointees also comprise the whole of the employer team in JIC negotiations despite their heavy reliance on government loans and grants.

In other cases such as education, health, and the civil service the decisions of the negotiating bodies must be promulgated by a circular or order issued by the minister. In all of these instances representatives of the minister sit on the national council, though in the case of the Burnham negotiations in respect to teacher salaries the Department of Education and Science is "not constitutionally represented, but officials attend meetings of the committees to offer any information and advice which may be required and to provide secretarial assistance."

In all aspects of public expenditure a particular minister carries a responsibility to Parliament and at least once a year (usually more often) has to present estimates of expenditure for his sector of employment to the House of Commons. In the case of the local authorities and public corporations these amount to consolidated grants or loans in which labour costs are not itemised. Without the powers of ratification which he possesses elsewhere, the minister has little constraint on the result of such negotiations. The local powers to raise revenue on their own account make it difficult for any central body to exercise control over local authorities despite the formal powers possessed by the National Joint Council in the implementation of agreements. For example, there is plentiful evidence of "grade drift" in earnings among local authority employees who are being attracted to or maintained in jobs which are upgraded solely for the purpose of increasing the incumbents' earnings.

In recent years government attitudes toward the scope and methods of negotiation have been undergoing a transformation as the full realisation of the extent to which the government's role as the nation's largest employer coincided with its role as economic manager has become plain. The effect that alterations in government expenditure could have on the level of effective demand in the economy has been well learnt by past Keynesian governments in Britain. The sources of cost-induced inflation took a little longer to discover and have still to be effectively remedied. It was always clear that cuts in public expenditure had usually to lead in any government-imposed economies directed at reducing overall demand, but what was not really appreciated was the effect of traditional public service methods of wage negotiations in stimulating cost inflation.

Stemming from the "good employer" concept has come another, that of "fair comparisons" in earnings, i.e. comparisons with what employees in the private sector are earning. Since the report of the Priestley Commission in 1955, comparability has been refined and systematised in the work of the Civil

Service Pay Research Unit. Although Priestley was reporting on the civil service his general philosophy applies to the whole of the public services. "If the government, which represents him, pays what other responsible employers pay for comparable work the citizen cannot reasonably complain that he is being exploited. [The civil servant] cannot legitimately complain of injustice when his remuneration and conditions of service taken together approximate to those prevailing in the outside world." Comparability is seen to protect the taxpayer against overpaying the public servant while ensuring that the government employee is receiving his economic transfer wage.

What is not ensured, at any rate not by the pay research techniques used in the civil service nor by the crude comparisons of statistical averages used elsewhere in the public services, is that similar levels of productivity are being achieved in all situations. Moreover, even if this were so the comparability method sometimes leads to a situation in which the pay and conditions being earned by a small enclave of workers is transferred in toto to the different and many times greater work force of the public service. In many instances, therefore, pay comparisons of the kind now practised may quite easily lead to an almost random choice of analogue being magnified many times over in public employment. Within the public sector itself the national civil service has tended to be a guide to changes in earnings in local ·government, and those changes in the latter are then transferred to the health services and education. Two standing review bodies for senior employees in the civil service and health service have both used increases elsewhere in the public service as reasons for increasing the pay of higher civil servants and for doctors and dentists respectively.

Although increases in pay on the basis of comparability were allowed under the prices and incomes policy this was only where "the pay of a certain group has fallen seriously, and must not be used to spread pay increases into areas of employment where the original justication does not apply."[1] Instead the Prices and Incomes Board put forward a number of sugges-

1. White Paper "Prices and Incomes Policy after June 30, 1967." HMSO, Cmnd. 3235, para. 38.

tions for productivity-related wage bargains in local and national government employment to take the place of awards based on comparisons with earnings outside the public sector.

These suggestions, made in the context of overall government restraints on wage or salary increases, have had some effect upon the content of negotiations within public employment, particularly in the Post Office, but they have also served to increase uncertainty and have brought a new aggression to negotiating tactics. For public employees the use of "fair comparisons" has come to be seen as a fundamental principle of equity and these government restraints to be a challenge to their bargaining position, by removing their major negotiating plank. This uncertainty is reflected in the role of the minister vis-a-vis the Whitley or other negotiating machinery, and particularly in the decline of arbitration as a court of last resort. In those services in which the minister has had powers to veto or to delay the payment of Whitley awards, the viability of the constitution and procedure of the machinery has come under severe strain. Within the constitution or proceedings of most Whitley Councils there is a reference to decisions of the Council being implemented in such a manner as to "have regard to the public interest." It is around the definition of this public interest that most of the recent controversy has centred.

Industrial Relations in the Civil Service

THE OCCUPATIONAL STRUCTURE OF THE SERVICE

THE working definition of a civil servant is normally taken to be that of the Royal Commission of 1929-31 (Tomlin), namely "those servants of the Crown, other than holders of political or judicial offices, who are employed in a civil capacity, and whose remuneration is paid wholly and directly out of monies voted by Parliament."

In 1968 these comprised some 1,113,605 employees or 5 percent of the total employed work force. Of these 235,000 were working in manual or "industrial" employment located in widely varying establishments in engineering, shipbuilding, building and construction, etc. Another 417,000 worked in the Post Office and have subsequently given up civil service status. The largest proportion, 465,000, were nonindustrial civil servants based in the U.K. It is upon the staff-management relations in this section of public employment that this chapter concentrates. In the year ending March 1967 the wages and salaries bill for these and for white-collar employees in the Post Office was £840 million or 12 percent of total public expenditure on salaries and wages in that year.

The modern civil service is generally held to have been started by the order in council of May 21, 1855, which set up the Civil Service Commission to conduct "the examination of the young men proposed to be appointed to any of the junior situations in the Civil Establishments." The order resulted from a report commissioned by Gladstone, who had appointed Sir Charles Trevelyan, the Under-Secretary (permanent head) to the Treasury, and his political counterpart at the Board of Trade to inquire into the organisation of and recruitment to the permanent civil service. Fifty years before this, financial reforms making departmental heads accountable to the Commons for their expenditure had led to the adoption of entrance tests in many departments. Even so patronage remained widespread in 1855, and the Northcote-Trevelyan report suggested that a universal and uniform system of entrance examinations should be instituted for all classes. It further suggested that to "encourage industry and foster merit" among employees promotion channels should be provided for properly qualified officers. To mitigate

Table 1.

Civil Service Employees by Group, 1967

Staff Group	Permanent	Temporary	Total
Administrative	2,624	160	2,784
Executive (general and departmental)	87,907	3,159	91,066
Clerical officers (general and departmental)	117,308	22,869	140,177
Clerical assistants	35,419	53,849	89,268
Typing	11,079	18,880	29,959
Inspectorate	2,785	93	2,878
Messengerial	19,039	16,361	35,400
Professional, scientific, and technical I	20,518	6,000	26,518
Professional, scientific, and technical II	42,343	16,803	59,146
Ancillary, technical, and miscellaneous supervisory grades, etc.	38,085	17,877	55,962
	377,107	156,051	533,158

Source: Report of the Lord Fulton Committee, The Civil Service, Vol. 4, Factual, Statistical and Explanatory Papers. HMSO, 1968, p. 12.

the evils of existing fragmentation the report suggested that all first appointments should be placed on a uniform footing, that promotion should be made possible between as well as within departments, and that a universal grade of "supplementary clerks" should be created.

This scheme was never wholly realised, but the broad outlines of the centralised general class structure with overall control divided between the Civil Service Commission and the Establishments Division of the Treasury came into existence after the publication of the Reorganisation Committee Report of 1920. Patronage died out almost completely in the home civil service after an order in council of 1870 made competitive tests obligatory in home departments. Such examinations together with all other tests of fitness were made a Treasury responsibility and thereby established this department as the administrative as well as financial point of control within the service. Following the Playfair Commission in 1876, a common grading system consisting of administrative officers, higher division clerks, lower division clerks, and boy clerks was created. A common grade for writers engaged in mechanical clerical duties had already been established in 1871. Following the report of the Ridley Commission in 1890, uniformity of salaries and conditions throughout the civil service was introduced except in the administrative class (first division).

Throughout the history of the service most of the periodic commissions or committees of inquiry have been anxious to establish a body of senior civil servants in the administrative classes who were able to advise politicians in national decision-making free of any particular bias, be that bias stemming from political prejudice or even a learned bias of technical expertise. The classical traditions of Oxford and Cambridge have retained a pre-eminence in British public thought, and since these universities pioneered competitive examinations in the early nineteenth century they maintained their traditional control over the supply of educated entrants to the political and professional elites during the nineteenth century. The first three commissioners were graduates of these universities, and they set out to compete with other embryo professions for the products of the public schools and universities, offering, not a narrow field of specialisation, but a career for the "all-round man." Their growing success in obtaining long lists of applicants from the older universities was a mark of the early stamp of identity placed on the service. The image of the classically trained and literate civil servant is one which still permeates the service and can even be found in the laboriously stylised articles in many modern staff association magazines. Classical allusions are still frequent in government reports upon the most technically exact subjects.

In a very real sense this ethos has provided a legitimating and reinforcing ideology for the development of a system of the most broadly defined categories of work within which officers are expected to undertake a whole series of widely varying jobs during the course of their career. That there should be a universal categorisation for the purposes of pay and conditions follows inevitably as one of the primary objectives of centralisation. But for the better part of a century the Treasury has retained the means to fulfill its manpower requirements in each new specialist area of administration thrown up by interventionist government policies by drafting in "all-purpose" civil servants to provide the new function.

The clerical assistant class (typically women) is still, as in 1920, employed in "large blocks of simple routine work," the general clerical class in "dealing with particular cases in accordance with well defined regulations, instructions or general practice." The general executive class covers seven in-class grades and constitutes every middle management position from supervisor to head of a major executive establishment. The former nomenclature may be a misnomer, because often supervisory duties are not regarded as paramount among the tasks of an executive officer and clear cut distinctions between "policy work" and "executive work" are not often found at even the most junior levels of this grade. Certainly this is so within the administrative class, whose duties include both the formulation of policy, the coordination and improvement of government machinery, and the general administration and control of public departments. In practice the diversity of tasks performed within each class is often greater than that existing between classes; the relationship between the nationally agreed scales of remuneration and value of work performed is therefore sometimes a rather tenuous one.

The numbers of main classes have considerably increased since 1920 and now number 47. The scientific and scientific assistants classes were established in 1931, and in 1946 the general service professional class was set up. Most of the subsequent classes have become more and more specific to the skills or tasks of the occupants, the latest being that of the economist class in 1965. But most of these subsequent general classes have been employed in advisory or "staff" functions servicing the administrative or higher executive grades.

The selection and certification of candidates for permanent posts is, then, in the hands of the Commission, and for this purpose often competitive examinations are held at regular intervals during the year for the executive and administrative classes. In practice the use of internal promotion procedures has supplied an increasing number of officers to both classes, and the majority of the current intake to the executive class are promotees or have been successful in competitive tests limited to clerical officers. At clerical level there is open recruitment by means of educational qualification (general certificate of education), but once more entrance by way of promotion from the lesser qualified assistant clerical class is becoming increasingly normal in tight labour markets.

Despite the tendency towards departmental autonomy in promotion and recruitment policies, departments still rely heavily on the Commission to provide higher grade entrants and to confirm the first appointments of all their staff. But outside of these general service grades about 27 percent of the home civil service are employed in special departmental grades. These are grades which in the historical process of interdepartmental battles with the forces of centralisation (largely contained in Treasury and the general service staff associations) have successfully argued the existence of specialist administrative functions or the need for technical expertise within their staff. The largest employers of such specialist staff are the Department of Inland Revenue with 24,000 and the Department of Employment and Productivity (DEP) with 22,000. In both of these instances the main departmental classes have equivalent or very similar grades to those of the clerical and executive classes but do not have this class division. At administrative level the DEP is served by entrants to the general service class, while in Inland Revenue the inspectorate grade takes in higher executive and administrative level appointments.

These and all the 1,400 miscellaneous departmental grades have their terms and conditions of appointment determined locally subject to the approval of the Commission. More importantly, changes in the conditions of their appointment are also made at department level subject to confirmation by the Establishments

Division of the Treasury. The functions of both the Commission and the Establishments Division were passed into the hands of a newly established Civil Service Department in November 1968.

THE STATUS OF THE CIVIL SERVANT

Technically the civil servant's legal status remains as it was at the close of the eighteenth century, that is he is a servant of the Queen, dismissible at her pleasure. Even if he has (as many recently appointed policy advisers have) a contract of employment he cannot sue for wrongful dismissal unless he is protected by an act of Parliament. Technically, his tenure of office is as insecure as it was two hundred years ago when civil servants followed their political masters "into the wilderness" at the end of a term of office. In fact, however, the status of the "permanent" or "established" civil servant is possibly as secure as any in existence in Britain today.

This status is gained by achieving a certificate of "permanent employment" from the Civil Service Commission, now part of the Civil Service Department. This certificate is granted to nonindustrial civil servants of typist machine operator class and above after passing the prescribed tests of proficiency and serving a probationary period which taken overall is about six months. In the case of manipulative grades, such as porters and messengers, or the industrial civil servant, entrance tests are usually not required and the probationary period is of approximately two years in length. All other requirements in respect to age limits of certain appointments, health, character, and regularity of attendance are taken into account before certification.

From the commissioners' point of view any post which is likely to continue for a substantial period of time is regarded as permanent, and they "normally" regard it as their duty to test persons if they are likely to stay on until retirement. Those failing the medical examination may be granted permanent unestablished posts. However, in modern times the number of "temporary" civil servants has grown tremendously, and as can be seen in Table I above they constitute the major part of the lower grades, especially in typing. At one stage most promotions and transfers required recertification, but in some grades it is now possible to be promoted from one temporary grade to another.

Naturally this is an issue which concerns staff associations because certification is their major means to controlling entry to the labour market. With a constantly rising turnover of staff their degree of organisation and bargaining position is threatened. However, the major importance of certification is that it is the sole qualification for entrance to the noncontributory civil service superannuation fund (aside from holding an appointment direct from the Crown under the Superannuation Act 1965). The civil servant has no legal right to a superannuation allowance, but unless he is dismissed or resigns before age fifty he receives a pension at age sixty-five (sixty for women) normally based on his salary over his total length of service.

As well as these benefits the status of a civil servant implies wide responsibilities under a number of blanket provisions which greatly affect his right as a citizen.

> The first duty of a civil servant is to give his undivided allegiance to the State. . . . He must not put himself in a position where his duty and his private interests conflict. . . . [His] private activities . . . must not be such as might bring discredit on the Service. . . . He must not lay himself open to suspicion of dishonesty. . . . Civil servants who advise Ministers and carry out Ministers' policies . . . should not normally take an active part in any matter which is, or could be, one of public and political controversy, whether or not it is one with which they are officially concerned. (Treasury Regulations, Establishment Code, Ka 2.)

These general provisions made in 1928 have subsequently been detailed in regulations relating to duties relating to the respect of the rights of the citizen, the handling of contracts, the acceptance of gifts or rewards, the holding of company stock and other external sources of income, and publication of information or opinions. These regulations extend to procedures to be adopted when a civil servant is involved in civil or criminal actions at law.

Since the middle of the last century when Crown servants campaigned for the right to vote, the most controversial restrictions on civil servants are those on the political activities. After the general strike in 1926 the government severely restricted the civil rights of civil servants, and all nonindustrial civil servants were forbidden to stand for Parliament. In 1948 the postwar Labour administration appointed a committee to examine the limitations placed upon civil servants' political rights. This report, discussed in the Whitley Council, eventually resulted in a threefold division of the service.

1. All industrial staff, minor and manipulative grades, and other grades determined departmentally are virtually free to take part in any form of political activity.

2. An intermediate group are free to engage in most political activities subject to certain conditions including permission from their departmental head. These include most grades above those above and up to and including the executive class. They are not, however, free to become parliamentary candidates and a "code of discretion" is imposed upon all their actions.

3. Senior civil servants are debarred from national politics but can seek permission to engage in local authority politics.

For staff associations which rely on parliamentary pressure group tactics in many areas of negotiation and for those affiliated to the politically conscious TUC these restrictions are irksome and are often criticized. Civil servants in the second and third categories who resign in order to take a parliamentary candidature are not entitled to reinstatement.

THE DEVELOPMENT OF COLLECTIVE BARGAINING

The reforms to the structure of the civil service during the latter half of the nineteenth century were not unaffected by collective representation on behalf of nonindustrial staff. Departmental grades in the Post Office and Inland Revenue were the first to organise successful combinations, which was done as early as 1858. These grades had submitted "humble petitions" to the heads of their departments and later combined this approach with parliamentary lobbying. The introduction of general service conditions in 1890 allowed a wider sense of group identification and of common grievance among all classes. But in 1871 the lowest grade of clerk, the writer, was given permanent status concurrently with becoming the first general class employed on uniform conditions. The deprivation felt by those who had *not* been given this status provided the initial impetus to protest, but the low level of pay, the lack of future prospects, and the constant alteration of regulations without improvements in conditions were seen by the Playfair Commission (1875) as the reason for continuing clerical unionism. A Treasury minute of February 1864 declared that "it is far from the desire of Her Majesty's Government that any classes of public servants or any individuals should be debarred from making a respectful representation in regard to any matter in which they may feel aggrieved and My Lords will always be prepared to give every consideration," but submission through the head of department was required. In 1880 a group of second division clerks who were later to form a permanent association successfully petitioned the Treasury over the heads of their department for a pay raise. This association reverted to departmental claims after a second attempt at petitioning the Treasury, but a new lower-class association, the Assistants Clerks Association, began a series of regular interchanges with the Treasury in 1905. Up to 1911 both the ACA and the Second Division Clerks Association submitted claims to the Treasury.

Other associations for women clerks, typists, and boy clerks were in existence at the turn of the century. In 1903, 90 percent of the 601 women typists were unionised; by 1912 a similar proportion of the 2,400 male clerks were in the ACA. By 1914 there were 73 active associations in the civil service with a membership varying between 75 percent and 100 percent of the groups being organised. Official attitudes to staff association membership varied within departments, but at no time was union membership officially prohibited. Treasury officials made discouraging statements and did not generally respond directly to association requests but put changes into operation thereafter.

This was the situation up to 1911 when, as a result of a series of ad hoc changes to terms and conditions of various classes, a number of anomalies appeared, and Treasury refused to entertain any further representations from the associations. In this year major organisational changes affecting the main departmental grades highlighted still existing patronage in these and other places. A protest meeting in which several public service unions participated was held and a sustained lobbying campaign began. This activity led to the formation of a federation of the 22 largest associations. The new federation took up an existing demand for an all-service Court of Appeal consisting of a panel of arbitrators to judge the merit of claims the Treasury refused to entertain. Their immediate objective was a general inquiry into the service, and this was achieved in the MacDonnell Commission created in 1912. It reported in 1914 and many of its recommendations were subsequently taken up in the postwar Reorganisation Committee proposals.

The federation was not a very effective body, but it provided a focus for the demands of its more militant affiliates such as the ACA and the postal and telegraphic associations in their attempts to break wartime income restraints. In 1917 it was successful in bringing about the establishment of a "permanent" tribunal, the Conciliation and Arbitration Board. This board consisted of an independent chairman and three representatives (not a member of the class in question) from each side. Its terms of reference were to examine pay claims from all nonindustrial civil servants whose salary range had a maximum of less than £500. In claims referred to it by either side the board was to assure itself that an adequate process of negotiations had preceded the reference followed by an attempt to conciliate between the parties. Only after conciliation had failed was the claim to be officially presented as one in which the board should arbitrate.

This board remained in existence until 1922 when a Committee of Government Expenditure ended it for reasons of economy. In a concurrent announcement the Treasury said that arbitration was "contrary to the spirit and intention of Whitleyism." After considerable agitation by staff side associations, arbitration was restored in 1925 without the former conciliation phase.

In 1917 a rift appeared in the Civil Service Federation between the postal and telegraphic associations and the clerical association over a separately negotiated increase granted to the former. The clerical associations then formed a separate federation, the Civil Service Alliance. During that year the Reconstruction Committee appointed by the war cabinet published a report on the future of industrial relations. This report, known by the name of the committee's chairman, the Right Honourable J. H. Whitley, M.P., put forward the notion of Joint Industrial Councils at all levels of private industry, each of which on its own level would assume the task of promoting industrial harmony and efficiency through consultation and negotiation at regular and frequent intervals. The Civil Service Alliance immediately began a campaign for a similar structure within the service and were rewarded by the support of a second report by the Whitley Committee. The principle was accepted by the Chancellor of the Exchequer but passed to a parliamentary committee for drafting. In 1919 this committee came forward with the suggestion that Whitley machinery might be used to improve efficiency and organisation but consideration of matters appertaining to the terms and conditions of employment could only be of a consultative kind. "The fact that the State is the ultimate employer of Government servants through the Heads of Departments who consequently have not the freedom of decision in regard to wages and conditions enjoyed by the private employer"[1] was regarded as reason to conclude that ministerial control must remain unimpaired.

A joint meeting of the associations and government officials was called where it was proposed by the secretary of the Postmen's Federation that a provisional National Joint Com-

1. Sir T. Heath Committee, *Report on the Application of the Whitley Report to the Administrative Departments, etc.* Cmnd. 9 (1919), para. 7.

mittee should be formed to reconsider the main principles of the proposed Whitley machinery and to draw up a detailed scheme for its implementation. This proposal was accepted by the Chancellor of the Exchequer who was present and the provisional committee formed thereafter drafted a constitution which remains largely unaltered today. The staff side proposal was tactically very sound but the Chancellor's acceptance was quite obviously influenced by the desire of the government to set an example in a potentially volatile situation. For years before and during the war, civil service unionism had been influenced by a growing militancy among shop stewards in private industry. The campaign for Whitleyism was paralleled by a staff association campaign to provide jobs "fit for heroes" who were returning from the war. Above all the spectre of Bolshevism was very real at that time and for some years to come. Rather than suppressing these forces the Treasury showed the same willingness to bend to them and to make use of them for the purposes of central public administration that they had displayed in their approach to the earlier representations from staff associations.

THE WHITLEY STRUCTURE IN THE NONINDUSTRIAL CIVIL SERVICE

The concept of Whitleyism arises out of proposals of the report presented to Parliament in 1917 by the Post War Reconstruction Committee. The emphasis in the definition of such systems is upon cooperation between staff and management rather than upon negotiation between two sides. Many industries have adopted the model and the point of emphasis in negotiation or cooperation varies between one industry and another. Basically all councils of the Whitley type fulfil the same function as most orthodox collective bargaining machinery. They exist to set the substantive and procedural rules of work relations through a process of negotiating between management and labour from separate power bases, and through management consultation with the representatives of labour. In event of failure to agree, there is normally resort to a special arbitration court at the request of one party but with the agreement of the other, rather than reliance upon external sanctions. They may have separate procedures for individual grievances but it is quite usual to resolve such grievances within the Whitley Council itself. If Whitleyism is to be seen as being in any way different from orthodox bargaining the differences lie in the scope and nature of negotiations and in the approach of the two sides to the process.

The structure and form of the civil service Whitley system reflects more accurately than any other Joint Industrial Council now in existence the spirit and intentions of the authors of the 1917 report. The Council set up in July 1919 has weathered many changes in the make-up of its constituents and most recently their members have been reduced from 54 to 52 as a result of changes following the separation of the Post Office from the civil service on November 1, 1969. Its constitution has, however, remained virtually unchanged since 1919. The objects of the National Council are set out in its constitution as being those of "securing the greatest measure of cooperation between the State in its capacity as employer, and the general body of Civil Servants in matters affecting the Civil Service; with a view to increased efficiency in the public service combined with the well-being of the employed to provide machinery for dealing with grievances and generally to bring together the experience and different points of view of representatives of the administrative, clerical and manipulative Civil Service." In the degree to which it succeeds in achieving these objectives, it and the whole structure of departmental and office committees are probably unique in the U.K.

The composition of each side is a matter entirely for itself to decide. The head of the civil service is normally chairman of the National Council, but in any case an official side representative is always in the chair at all levels of the Whitley structure, though the title of vice-chairman is carried by the chairman of staff side. The official side now consists of 24 members including the permanent heads of the major departments, representatives of the Civil Service Department (these are also the chief negotiators in meetings with individual staff associations) and the permanent head of the Treasury. Members often continue to serve in a personal capacity after moving from one department to another. The official side were initially chosen by the Cabinet, but up to 1968 the successors to the first Council had been invited to join by the Treasury. Now such invitations are extended by the Civil Service Department in consultation with the Treasury. Staff side consists of 28 members including the chairman, secretary general, secretary, and assistant secretary of the staff side federal body. The staff side was originally appointed by the major groups of associations in existence in 1919 and this method of appointment was embodied in the constitution. Either side may appoint persons of standing (who may or may not be civil servants); in practice this clause enables full-time officials of staff associations to represent their members on both national and departmental councils. Members of the national official side are now invariably serving civil servants: from 1922 till 1930 the official side included three Members of Parliament (from the government), but the practice was dropped on the recommendation of a Royal Commission in 1931 for reasons stemming from the desire to keep the service free from direct political influence and in order that a Cabinet decision on Whitley recommendations could be taken free from any prior commitment on the part of its representatives on the Council. In other words, there was a desire that ultimate Cabinet responsibility should remain unimpaired.

Questions discussed at Whitley Councils or Committees are not settled by a vote; each side speaks formally as a whole although freedom is allowed for informal initiatives by individual members. There are no formal standing orders or rules of procedure though in fact the methods of promulgation of decisions and the uses of precedent provide a well understood style and order of business. Nonetheless most business is advanced informally by frequent informal communications between the Civil Service Department (formerly the Establishments Division at the Treasury) and the permanent secretariat of the Whitley staff side.

The full National Whitley Council (NWC) may meet once a quarter according to its constitution. This practice was abandoned at the outbreak of World War II, and subsequently such meetings have been infrequent. Instead formal business is carried in two standing committees and a number of ad hoc ones. On Committee A, more senior members of both sides discuss substantive issues concerning major changes in remuneration or important procedural modifications. Committee **B** is largely concerned with fringe benefits and working conditions although major matters of policy such as the geographical dispersion of departments or computerisation have begun to be discussed in this committee. However, both these and similar matters were dealt with in one of the many subcommittees which service these two major committees before appearing on the agenda of either. Neither committee has formal terms of reference. Their composition on the official side is largely confined to Civil Service Department and sometimes Treasury officials.

Since 1919 departmental councils (DWCs) have come into being along similar lines, though each has been subjected to frequent disintegration and reformation as successive governments have dissolved old ministries and created new ones to accord with the prevailing parliamentary view of public policy or administration. There are now 70 in existence. Each departmental staff side is appointed in the first place by the associations represented in the department, which are called together for the purpose by the head of the department. It is taken to be "natural and logical to confine such a meeting to recognised associations, in which case presumably recognised associations only could be represented on the Staff Side as first constituted, but thereafter the filling of vacancies would be left entirely to the Staff Side itself."[2]

Both levels of Whitley machinery, national and departmental, have a defined field of activity. Nationally the agenda consists of general issues or those having generalisable implications; departmental items are specific to that level alone, but they can involve the working out of a general agreement in terms of its departmental application. Questions concerning two or

2. H.M. Treasury, *Staff Relations in the Civil Service,* HMSO, 1965, para. 15, p. 8.

more departments are reported to the NWC. Generally the National Council is not seen as a court of appeal for issues arising with departmental councils; the advice of the NWC is often sought but decisions are thereafter taken within the DWC. Clearly on matters involving heavy increases in departmental expenditure the parallel channel of communication within the governmental machinery and subsequent informal meetings with national officials of the staff associations involved, modify the reality of the formal powers of departments. In these matters the status of the official side of the DWC in the compilation of the civil estimates is most important. Before its separation many agreements made in the Post Office DWC had extremely important implications for total civil expenditure and the same is true for a lesser extent of other major departmental grades such as inland revenue.

One of the more important powers of the departmental council is that of establishing district or office (or works) committees. Under the provisions of the initial application of the Whitley Report to administrative departments (Cmnd. 198) these may be set up in establishments employing sufficient officers or where establishments are not large enough for such a committee to be established they may be set up to cover a number of establishments within the same department on a district basis. These committees consist of the establishment officer or officers responsible for the office or officers together with their section heads meeting with staff association representatives who are employed within that establishment or district. Full-time officers of the association or senior departmental representatives may be invited to participate where their help is required in settling some specific issue but normally business is carried on by the branch officers or some other elected lay representatives of the unions. Again it is the responsibility of the office manager to see that if a request is made by one staff association for the formation of a local Whitley Council, all other recognised associations in the office are informed of the intention. Often departments restrict the size of each staff side at local level to two or three times that of the official side.

Nothing in the constitution of the Whitley machinery prevents any staff association from negotiating on any issue on behalf of its own members alone. Clearly there must be a consensus among staff side over a wide range of issues and for this purpose a full-time Secretariat was established shortly after the first Whitley meeting. On the other hand many all-service awards are followed by individual staff association or departmental staff action to gain some favourable application of the award to the situation of their members. However, most pay claims are pursued independently as additions to anything obtained by way of staff side action.

ORGANISATION ON THE STAFF SIDE

Over 200 associations were represented on staff side in 1919 through federations or occupational groupings, the number of seats being based loosely on consideration of the number of persons in the class represented and the proportion of such persons in the union claiming representation on their behalf. By 1956 this number had declined to 25 and today (after the removal of Post Office unions) it is 12 plus 1 confederation.

As was brought out in the previous section, the provisions made for the composition of the staff side of the Whitley Council are such as to make it a largely self-perpetuating body. The members appointed by Cabinet authority in 1919 represent staff groupings which formed the basis for the future composition of the staff side, each change being dictated by already repre-sented bodies. Whether by reason of their early monopoly over the Whitley machinery or the continuing strength of the alle-giances of their members, the associations which are directly represented on the National Whitley machinery have approxi-mately 90 percent of civil servants in membership. Just over 3 percent are contained in associations which either brief another staff side association or have no links with the councils at all.

The allocation of the seats on staff side is shown below. Crudely speaking, association representation follows the occupa-tional class lines used within the service. Thus the Civil and Public Services Association represent the two clerical grades together with teleprinter operators and the bulk of secretaries, typists, and office machine operators. The latter groups are shared with other members of the Civil Service Alliance, who

Table 2.

National Staff Side, from January 1969

Associations represented	Seats	Number in post in grades for which Association was recognised in 1967
Civil Service Alliance		91,681
Civil and Public Services Associations (CPSA)	5	84,793
Inland Revenue Staff Federation (IRSF)	2	31,763
Ministry of Labour Staff Association (MLSA)	1	19,874
Country Courts Officers Association (CCOA)	1	5,248
Executive Group		
Society of Civil Servants (SCS)	3	52,963
Customs Group of Associations (CGA)	1	9,047
Association of Officers of the Ministry of Labour (AOML)	1	5,452
Association of H.M. Inspectors of Taxes (AIT)	1	2,180
CSU/POA Group		
Civil Service Union (CSU)	2	37,001
Prison Officers Association (POA)	1	10,764
IPCS/STCS		
Institution of Professional Civil Servants (IPCS)	3	77,310
Society of Technical Civil Servants (STCS)	1	8,685
Association of First Division Civil Servants (AFDCS)	1	5,842
Association of Govt. Supervisors & Radio Officers (AGSRO)	1	3,038
Subtotal	24	
Secretariat and Chairman of National Staff Side	4	
Total	28	

Source: National Staff Side Whitley Council and Factual Statistical and Explanatory Papers, Lord Fulton Committee on the Civil Service 1966-68, Vol. 4.

because of the departmental gradings of their members take in some grades who in the general ("Treasury") grades would be classified as executive class officers. The largest union is however the CPSA, whose numerically greater female membership in the common grades carries its membership strength up to about 181,000. Similarly the majority of executive level officers are to be found in the Society of Civil Servants with some departmental grades of more or less the same standing forming a loose alliance with the main grade union.

The only remaining civil service group to designate itself as a "union" is that for the manipulative, cleaning, and messengerial grades. In fact this union has recruited into its ranks many of the ancillary grades such as scientific instructional officers, radio technicians, and supervisors of manual workers who are also represented by minority associations and might well be grouped in the other major alliance (now merged), that of the Institution of Professional Civil Servants. The Institution, as its name implies, takes in all of the specialist classes of professional advisors created during this century. In addition, however, its jurisdiction covers many purely technician grades, and its current merger with the Society of Technical Civil Servants extends its coverage to all draughtsmen and the low graded tracers. The other association catering for technicians and supervisors is the Association of Government Supervisors and Radio Officers. The administrative class is covered by the Association of First Division Civil Servants.

Staff Side does not have the power to determine which union will be recognized by the government. The power of recognition is retained by the Civil Service Department at national level (the Treasury up to 1968) and in the heads of respective departments. The process of recognition is older than Whitleyism and a pledge was given by the government that recognised associations would continue to have the right of direct consultation, outside of the councils, on matters affecting their members alone.

Three other national associations are recognised, those for nationally employed police, lawyers, and fire officers. In addition, 22 departmental associations have no direct access to the Whitley machinery. These cover a great many departmental grades with a very small membership, a large noncivil service printing union with 40 civil service members and 3 of the staff sides in the health service who between them represent some 50 members in the national civil service.

As in other forms of public service relations recognition is a formal act. It enables participation in negotiations leading to agreements, to consultation, and to the use of the Civil Service Arbitration Tribunal. To secure recognition an association must show that it is representative and (outside of the Post Office) this has normally implied that it has to demonstrate that a large proportion of the grade for which recognition is claimed are in membership. For national recognition covering more than one department this must be demonstrated nationally, and departmentally, within the grade or part of the grade serving in that department for which recognition is claimed. The Treasury has never announced any precise percentages which would establish a claim to national recognition or act as a guide to departmental heads in recognising or withdrawing recognition from an association. Where conflicting claims occur or seem likely to occur, steps are taken to ascertain the paid-up membership before recognition is granted. Recognition may be withdrawn if membership figures change. Normally the initiative in claiming withdrawal is taken by a rival association, though there is nothing to prevent the establishment division from taking the initiative itself if the facts seem to justify an investigation of the current membership of recognised associations.

Recognition carries with it the privilege of special leave, time off and secondment (temporary assignment to other duties, including union office) for association representatives who are permanent civil servants. Leave and time off is related to attendance at Whitley Committees or on Whitley business carried out in staff association meetings. Secondment to the full time staff of national associations is quite usual in the case of civil servants who have been appointed to union office and are serving their probationary period with that association. Staff side secretaries at local level "should as far as possible be given light official duties" and all facilities to contact or communicate with members other than holding meetings in office hours are allowed. From 1966 onwards the departments have also undertaken to deduct subscriptions at source ("check-off") and all the larger associations now pay the government a commission to perform this service.

Whether recognition is granted nationally or at departmental level it covers only matters which are (1) within the competence of the recognising authority to settle with or without reference to higher authority and (2) domestic to the group in respect of which recognition is granted. There are a number of cases of joint recognition, particularly where a departmental association covers a major part of the staff in a particular grade and a national association covers the rest. Matters affecting such staff may be discussed jointly or separately with the associations concerned and on occasion separate agreements have been made. This has been permitted by the physical or geographical separation of bargaining units: little actual overlapping of jurisdiction occurs within the same place of work. It is much more common for the general service associations, prominently the CPSA and SCS, to have recruited equivalent grades in the Whitehall headquarters staff of a department to those which, in the provinces, are organised by a departmental association.

There have been three types of jurisdictional disputes arising out of the recognition policy pursued by the Treasury and departmental heads. The first is that alluded to above in which general service associations launched campaigns designed to bring about mergers with smaller intraclass or departmental associations. This type of campaign was attempted by the CPSA during the 1930s against the Inland Revenue Staff Federation, the Ministry of Labour Staff Federation and the County Court Officers Association. In 1939 it came to an end with the formation of a confederation between the four associations named the Civil Service Alliance. The Alliance executive committee meets regularly to form common policy on various issues and to finance a joint research department. Each partner has an obligation to keep the others informed of current and prospective movements affecting the pay and conditions of those they represent. The committee has power to decide whether proposed sectional claims or agreements shall be approved. It is a seemingly precarious relationship and in its evidence to the Donovan Commission the CPSA alleged that it, as the largest affiliate, had financed the survival of the two smaller members. The perceived higher stakes of these associations possibly explains why, despite possible disadvantages to their members in long run salary trends, these associations continue with little professional help outside of the Alliance.

Other organisations to have achieved recognition over long periods were special interest groups representing women officers and ex-servicemen (veterans associations). Both groups of membership had special grievances arising out of lower rates of salary than those being paid generally. Both were the particular concern of the CPSA within whose jurisdiction most of these groups fall. This association took the lead in mounting successful parliamentary lobbying by staff side on both issues. Equal pay for women and men in the nonindustrial civil service was gained by an act passed in 1955 and thereafter the last of these groups subsided. Some of them were breakaways in their origin and these still occur from time to time and manage to gain recognition. These have not been a problem since the subsidence of the women's movements except in the Post Office where the Union of Post Office Workers continues to experience such attempts at recognition on the part of recalcitrant minority groups.

A substantial part of present day negotiations is conducted through direct discussion between the government representatives and individual associations. A decision whether it should be conducted in Whitley or individual negotiations is entirely decided in the light of the situation. For the association not represented on a Whitley Council there is of course little choice but to enter into individual discussions with the CSD or the department. Because most single-grade pay changes are made through channels involving only individual associations and because they have complete access to arbitration procedures, such non-Whitley associations can make an effective representative body. In any case individual grievances cannot be taken up in Whitley so that over both individual as well as collective functional areas such smaller bodies can operate effectively. Although the odds are against non-Whitley unions it cannot be said that on balance those represented on the Whitley Council have a monopoly of resources or rights. Indeed it may well be that some of the larger associations *have* actually kept smaller associations in being. Most associations representing general service classes have agreed to safeguard the interests of associations representing intraclass or "linked-grade" employees in Whitley discussions. There is little doubt that like the CPSA in its relationship to the IRSF, MLSF and CCOA, they hoped that by doing so they might foster a permanent merger. The rather surprising result of the recent reshuffling of seats on staff side following the Post Office group's removal is that the CCOA has obtained direct representation for the first time.

The big advantage to be gained by representation on the National Council is to be found in the constant dialogue conducted on a wide range of subjects and in an informal manner with the employer representatives. This constant access to information and involvement in decision taking is made easier by the existence of a permanent secretariat for the staff side. The principal officers sit as permanent members of staff side and are in day to day contact or communication with CSD, Treasury or Cabinet officials. In a manner traditional to the civil service (and to many British trade unions) there has until recently been no specialist research function; this has now been added to the secretariat.

The head of this secretariat is the secretary general of staff side and it represents all staff associations in day to day business with the government. Beneath him is a secretary who is responsible for the agenda at the weekly meetings of staff side Committee A and the monthly meetings of Committee B. These parallel similar committees within Whitley, and ad hoc subcommittees are formed when the need arises. General secretaries of affiliated bodies usually attend Committee A, more junior officers attend Committee B. All minutes together with copies of important communications passed between the secretariat and government officers are circulated to affiliated organisations, and, in the manner of the civil service these take on a line of procedure which is constantly referred to inside and between staff associations.

The chairman of staff side is titular head. He is not

a full-time officer of the secretariat like the Secretary General, but is elected from among the association delegates to staff side. Perhaps as important as anything the secretariat actually does is the status and deference accorded to both the secretary general and chairman of staff side within the government. It is unusual for either to retire from their office without being offered some important departmental or other public service appointment. The present industrial relations director at the now independent Post Office Corporation is a former secretary general of staff side. In many ways the high personal standing enjoyed by staff side officials in industrial relations reflects the consensus in values and behaviour within the Whitehall-based civil service. The permanency of relationships and introversial manner in which substantive issues are viewed have tended to divorce the advances represented in Whitleyism from mainstream trends in other sectors and indeed even from Whitleyism in the industrial civil service. Yet this sense of corporate identity may well have helped to maintain the structure and quality of the Whitley concept at times when the highly articulated class divisions in the general service and the occupational identities of professional and technical groups became most evident in interunion struggles.

All of the associations left on staff side since the secession of the Post Office are first and foremost civil service in character, style, and organisation. Many of the internal procedures of the associations are modelled on those of the service to an extent that goes beyond the needs of alignment with the employers. It goes without saying that associations representing the managerial classes—the Society of Civil Servants and the Association of First Division Civil Servants—are somewhat less like unions in behaviour than the others. For a period the SCS attempted to restrict itself to promoting professional standards, and it is still true that the AFDCS prefers a professional approach to that of collective bargaining (the structure of decision-taking in regard to their remuneration allows this approach —see *Scope of Bargaining* below).

Like the main Post Office unions the lower grade associations in the civil service have always felt a greater affiliation to the labour movement outside the Service. As early as 1920 the

Clerical Officers Association (now CPSCA) had become affiliated to both the TUC and the Labour Party. The Tax Officers (IRSF) affiliated to the TUC, as did the major women's associations. The general strike in 1926 caused the immediate disaffiliation of the latter, although the General Purposes Committee (Committee A) of staff side instructed civil servants not to perform any other than their normal duties and not to volunteer for added work. This action caused the higher grade associations to split from the Whitley staff side for a period.

As a direct result of the general strike and the growing political involvement of some staff side leaders the government included in the Trades Disputes and Trades Unions Act 1927 a clause forbidding established civil servants from being members, delegates, or representatives of any trade union of which the membership was not confined to Crown employees. In addition they could not join organisations federated to other trade unions than civil service associations or associated directly or indirectly with any political party or organisation.[3]

The result was not such as to outwardly affect the political activity of the CPSA, (see *Dispute Settlement* below), and fraternal delegates continued to be exchanged between the TUC and former affiliates. It did, however, put the stamp of civil service insularity on staff associations for nearly twenty years up to 1946 when the act was repealed by the postwar Labour administration. In particular the Institution of Professional Civil Servants which had formerly had attachments to the industrially based Association of Scientific Workers and to other more professional bodies and the Society of Technical Civil Servants, which had formerly been virtually a wing of the Association of Engineering and Shipbuilding Draughtsmen, became totally autonomous organisations within the service. Hence in this one act the "purity" of staff side was assured and the basis for present traditions was laid. Not only was it cut off from the Labour movement but also from all professional associations and even international civil service organisations.

3. See Trades Disputes and Trade Union Act 1927, 17 and 18 George V, c. 22, cl. V.

Since the act was revoked, only the Union of Post Office Workers has reaffiliated to the Labour Party, but outside the Post Office, the CPSA, the IRSF, the MLSA, the CSU, the AGSRO and the Society of Technical Civil Servants have affiliated to the TUC. Since the latter has now merged with the much larger Professional Civil Servants who recently rejected TUC affiliation (against the advice of its executive), it seems likely that IPCS leadership will attempt to retain the STCS link with the TUC in the terms of the merger. In 1968 the CSU and the AGSRO used the mediating services of the TUC Bridlington procedures to sign a "spheres of influence" agreement in respect to Treasury and other grades without the Treasury being officially involved in any way.

Since the war the Civil Service Alliance has filled a seat on the General Council of the TUC and has taken a prominent part in general debates. The resolution which ended the 1949-50 "pay restraint" by the TUC was seconded by the CPSA general secretary, and throughout the 1960s that union took a lead in debates on incomes policy. This position reflects the perennial and rather narrow concern of public service unions with the more direct effect which incomes restraint has on salaries in their sector. In the 1940s some association leaders became prominent in advancing left-wing views on foreign policy, particularly during the cold war period. A growing concern with Communist infiltration of staff associations caused the Cabinet to issue a directive in 1950 that establishment officers should no longer negotiate with staff side representatives who were known to be Party members. This was a period of bitter intraunion factional disputes in most British organisations concentrated most prominently in the civil service within the CPSA. During the next decade the emphasis given to presenting an apolitical image resulted in a retrenchment and return to concern with nonindustrial civil service issues. No contact is maintained with unions in the industrial sector of the service, and any regular communication with them takes place at plant level only or within the TUC.

ORGANISATION AND AUTHORITY ON THE EMPLOYERS' SIDE

It is convenient to divide a discussion of the official side under three headings, first, the decision-making authority, that is, the process between Cabinet and Whitley Councils; second, the sources of finance which give powers of surveillance to the House of Commons; and last, the management and planning functions of the Civil Service Department as one of the largest single employers of labour in the U.K.

Decision-Making Authority

When Whitleyism was first proposed as a form of consultation the protest it evoked caused a change in the ultimate phrasing of the constitution of the National Council to provide that the functions of the Council should include "the determination of the general principles governing conditions of service," and "proposed legislation so far as it has a bearing on the position of Civil Servants in relation to their employment." It provided that the decisions of the Council "shall be arrived at by agreement between the two sides, shall be signed by the Chairman and Vice-Chairman, shall be reported to the Cabinet, and thereupon become operative."

The Tomlin Commission Report (1931, para. 495) interpreted this as meaning that "In fact the position is, and must remain, that, unless the Cabinet through Ministers authorises the Official Side to agree, no agreement can be reached on the Council." Hence in theory prior Cabinet or ministerial authority is required for the opening of Whitley discussions and/or the concluding of agreements; each minister standing in precisely the same position in regard to departmental official side as the Cabinet does to the national body.

In reality, agreements between the two sides are rarely "reported to the Cabinet," and a good deal of de facto power rests in the hands of the head of the civil service, the permanent secretary to the Treasury, and the secretary of the Cabinet. For the last century the history of the civil service has been largely made up of attempts by the Treasury to gain central authority over the structure and conditions of employment throughout the home civil service. This authority was formalised in Article 6 of the Civil Service Order in Council 1956 when the Treasury was empowered "to make regulations or give instructions for controlling the conduct of H.M. Home Civil Service." In practice the Treasury had been issuing circulars conveying instructions or guidance to departments since the introduction of uniform conditions of employment in the late nineteenth century. These were brought together in 1944 under the title of Estacode (Establishment Code) which, with all subsequent supplements and amendments, provides establishment officers throughout the service with a standing authority.

Within the Treasury a large and increasingly specialized management group has grown up in the postwar period. The oldest parts of this were those dealing with pay and pensions, and the establishment division. The latter were primarily responsible for formulating the principles and policy governing recruitment and establishment for which function it required to work in close collaboration with the Civil Service Commission, a body which for historical reasons remained separated from the Treasury. It was also concerned with overall staff needs, movements between departments. It offered advice to departmental heads and the establishment divisions existing within all major departments on these and other matters such as discipline, and what, in recent times, has come to be known by the title of "career development," though little has been accomplished.

In all such matters the Treasury view has been reflected by the nine Treasury members of the twenty-four on official side but more importantly by the predominance of its officials in the committees which carry out Whitley business. Treasury officials were also present in all important departmental discussions and in negotiations with individual staff associations. Treasury officials were in fact the chief negotiators for the official side. In this way, decisions were approved by the Treasury and the subsequent report to the Cabinet office was a somewhat formal process.

There have been exceptions to this rule, more recently in 1961 when under the terms of general income restraints the

Chancellor of the Exchequer prohibited agreements. Even more recently under the powers given to him by the Prices and Incomes Act the Minister for Economic Affairs referred an award of the Standing Advisory Committee for the Pay of Higher Civil Servants to the NBPI. In 1970 a subsequent award was halved on the authority of the Prime Minister himself.

Neither of the awards was by agreement with staff side, but were unilateral recommendations by a special standing review committee on the pay of senior civil servants. A long-term pay agreement made in the Whitley Council was overriden in 1967, but as in 1965 this was done under the special ministerial powers of the Prices and Incomes Act. For more positive evidence of the normative powers of the government to dishonour Whitley agreements one had to return to a case arising out of a 1961 pay pause. The Crown was sued by a Ministry of Works lift attendant for increments held back by the Chancellor's suspension of arbitrated awards. Lord Justice Gardiner dismissed the case in 1964 on the grounds that the Crown had no enforceable contract or obligation to its employees. As the Judge put it, the civil servant is legally in a position "approximating to slavery."

The criteria of "all-round excellence" which has prevailed in the service since its modern origins have increasingly come under attack in postwar years from many quarters both inside as well as outside the service. A committee of inquiry was set up in 1966 to "examine the structure, recruitment and management, including training of the Home Civil Service, and to make recommendations." One of the immediate results of the committee report[4] was the transfer of all functions concerning (1) the organisation and conduct of the civil service and civil service pay and conditions of service; (2) the approval of entrance competitions; (3) certain other statutory functions in relation to pay, superannuation, etc., in the *public sector* and vis-à-vis other public bodies to a newly created body to be known as the Civil Service Department. Thus the functions which had so lately been gained by the Treasury were combined

4. Lord Fulton Committee, *The Civil Service,* Volume One, Report of the Committee, 1966-1968, HMSO, 1968, Cmnd. 3638.

with those of the Commission in a separate and independent body. One of the existing joint permanent secretaries to the Treasury was placed in the new role of head of the civil service responsible directly to the Prime Minister and with similar status to that of the remaining Treasury head. The Lord Privy Seal, a permanent Cabinet office, was given political responsibility for the day-to-day operations of the service. The holder of this office answers questions on the service in the House of Lords; the Paymaster General, usually a non-Cabinet post, answers questions in the Commons.

The Committee's reasons for change will be examined later; what is primarily of interest is the possible line of separate development in control over the service when it has been moved from its former proximity with financial policy making and department audit. The movement has meant the removal of many very senior civil servants from the Treasury who carry with them a high personal reputation in the service. Nevertheless the Treasury "presence" in major Whitley discussions was, and still is, largely a reflection of its wide measure of de facto power to approve or disapprove of expenditure on civil service staff costs. While the Treasury remains represented on the official side of Whitley, its role is formally much less than before. The ultimate chain of authority to the Prime Minister through the Lord Privy Seal in the case of the Civil Service Department may prove to be less effective than the sorts of arguments advanced through the Chancellor, particularly in a period of continued general restraint over incomes.

Finances

The principal means used by the Treasury to extend its influence over civil service establishment has been through the procedure by which departments submit their annual estimates of future expenditure during the forthcoming year to the ultimate arbiters of Crown expenditure—the House of Commons. These are drawn up by each department in November and submitted to the Treasury. The ministerial head of the Treasury, the Chancellor of the Exchequer, has overall responsibility for compiling the national budget presented in the following April.

The estimates are discussed over the period November to February in talks which proceed at a number of different levels from departmental ministers downwards. The final estimates are put to the House of Commons in March, within the general heading of civil estimates. There are separate departmental heads and within these are contained separate heads for staff costs. Every head provides a separate topic for debate and a vote is taken on each.

The estimates are for a financial year beginning and ending on March 31 and any surplus on that day is lost to the department. During the course of the year only certain defined monies can be moved between subheads (virement) but these do not generally include monies intended for staff costs. In order to meet any additional expenditure in this respect an appropriation vote can be taken for specific items or supplementary estimates can be put to the House during December, February, or August. Additional funds have also on occasion been made available by revised estimates in July. In general there is a great measure of flexibility in the ability of Parliament to grant funds for staffing purposes. The second and complementary means to financing civil service expenditure is through the consolidated fund. This title does not describe a financial pool; it simply refers to all fixed charges granted by statute. Among these are the pensions and other superannuated benefits of civil servants which are all provided with an annual sum allocated by Parliament for this purpose.

There are, however, four procedural rules to be observed. (1) A proposal for changes in finances has to emanate from the Crown, which gives ministers a virtual monopoly of initiative in direct parliamentary expenditure. (2) All charges must be considered in committee before a vote is taken. The most important of these, the Supplies Committee, examines estimates before they are presented to the House. (3) All charges must be authorised by the House of Commons. (4) Not more than one stage of a finance bill can be considered in a day. The modern functions of Parliament have been described as "examination, criticism, and approval," and in spite of the time provision made in the last rule its ability to criticise the technically complex estimates that are presented to it throughout the year are limited. Other additional means of scrutiny exist. For example, a special memorandum on the costs of civil service administration may be presented in the March estimates. More important, there are committees of the House with defined powers of inquiry and scrutiny. These are the Committee of Public Accounts, the Estimates Committee, and the Select Committee on Nationalised Industries. Of these the largest and most influential in civil service terms is the Estimates Committee.

This committee is one of the more important instruments of change within the House of Commons. In 1946/47 it encouraged the use of new management techniques in the civil service and in 1963/64 it suggested fundamental modifications to the Establishments Division. In addition it has made suggestions to the Commission on its recruitment methods. In 1957/58 it found the Treasury checks on departmental expenditure to be weak and ineffective and it urged development of forward programming. Its suggestions led on to a special committee of inquiry and it is in this respect that the committee operates to initiate concern with longer term issues such as the structural reform of the civil service. However ineffective Treasury control over general departmental expenditure, it has attempted to exercise control over staff costs by the imposition of the general normative restraints set by incomes policy in 1961/62 and again in 1966/70. General control over the national economy has over some years been passing out of Treasury hands. This has been largely because the Labour government identified the Treasury functions as being largely a restrictionist accountancy one: its senior economists were identified with the use of orthodox monetary control as an instrument of policy complemented by the negative and revenue-raising functions of the fiscal policy. Since that time circumstances and the internal political strength of the Treasury have brought the demise of the planning and coordinating ministry (DEA) set up in 1964. Yet the Department of Employment and Productivity has arisen to fulfil many of the interventionist tasks intended for the latter including the maintenance of incomes policy. The internal role of the Treasury in imposing the "norms" for pay increases set by the Chancellor (until July 1970 when the new Conservative Secretary for Employment announced changes!) upon its own staff has therefore been made somewhat more difficult since they no longer have overall responsibility for incomes policy. The result has been that a "tough line" adopted by the official side of National Whitley throughout the period of "freeze" and "restraint" has not always been reflected in private industry. This has created a growing resentment on staff side and increasing alienation from the traditional Whitley approach of cooperative bargaining and consultation.

The Personnel Management Function

All matters relating to staff and to conditions of work were dealt with by the management group of the Treasury, and within major departments the division of labour within this group was reflected in similar organisations. Broadly speaking, these consisted of pay and pensions, establishments, training, management services, and welfare. The first two functions are the oldest and best established and are generally reflected within the managerial functions at departmental level. Below this level the staff management function is generally considered a part of the duties of a senior officer or officers within each plant or office. Hence for convenience all matters pertaining to pay and conditions accrue to a single senior establishments officer in a large employing unit. At no point from the Treasury management group downwards have any management functions been considered specialties. Each job is undertaken as part of a wider range of jobs undertaken by a nonspecialist in the course of a civil service career. The management function is so little emphasized in the work role of the officer that the point is reached where a seventeen-year-old recruit to the executive grade can be given immediate supervisory responsibility over an office consisting of older but less senior staff.

This has long been recognised by staff associations which hold that junior grades are obstructive to good working relationships at the office level. In its evidence to the Fulton Committee the largest of these—the Civil and Public Service Association—suggested the development of a separate personnel function centered upon a department that was independent of the Treasury. An independent management consultancy employed by the Fulton Committee affirmed a need for such specialisation (see Volume Two of the Fulton Report). Their report suggested that Whitleyism had very little direct impact on the day-to-day operation of the civil service office establishment although joint consultation had facilitated wider changes within the service. At national level senior civil servants nevertheless placed an emphasis on the role as advisers to the government rather than as administrators.

The creation of the Civil Service Department is intended to represent a solution to the problem. First among its specific functions is that of personnel management and the development and dissemination of administrative and managerial techniques. So far the steps taken by Joint Committee on Fulton set up within the Whitley structure have been confined to an examination of present personnel management practices conducted by the department itself.

The current official attitude toward staff associations is to be found in the "Handbook for the New Civil Servant" given to every new recruit:

> You are not only allowed but encouraged to belong to a staff association. Besides being a good thing for the individual Civil Servant to belong to an association, which can support him in his reasonable claims and put his point of view before the authorities on all kinds of questions affecting his conditions of service, it is also a good thing for Departments and for the Civil Service as a whole that Civil Servants should be strongly organised in representative bodies. It is only commonsense to meet the wishes of the Civil Servant about his conditions of service as far as possible, for a contented staff will work much more efficiently than a staff which feels that its interests are being completely ignored by the "management."

More generally it is possible to distinguish an approach by official side to Whitley consultations which is more like that of more enlightened employers. The civil service management have certain tasks to accomplish in carrying out public policy (wherever it is generated). Its budgeting constraints are not very different from those applying in a large corporation; they can "afford" to consult extensively with their staff. In respect to nonindustrial civil servants, management is dealing with employee representatives who are moulded by the same rather insulated environment as that which is shaping their own attitudes and behaviour. To that extent the atmosphere in which consultation has taken place has gone far beyond that which has so far been obtained in the private sector. Nevertheless the 1919 Whitley agreement emphasized that the "public interest" constitutes a legitimate check on their rights and powers and official side have used this to claim management prerogatives on numerous occasions. In practice, however, it has never refused to discuss an issue in postwar years; nor has the government ever rejected a Whitley agreement nor been accused of breaking an agreement *except* under the provisions of incomes restraints which were general to all sectors of employment. This problem arose when the 1964 long-term agreement guaranteeing annual wage increases was abrogated in 1966 under the Prices and Incomes Act of that year.

THE SCOPE OF BARGAINING

The constitution of all Whitley Committees lays down that "The scope of the council shall compromise all matters which affect the conditions of service of the staff." The staff referred to are nonindustrial civil servants up to the lower administrative level, the remuneration of the managerial executive grades above this being excluded. Little else of relevance is excluded from discussion. Part (d) III of the constitution defines one function of the council as being the "determination of the general principles governing conditions of service, e.g. recruitment, hours, promotion, discipline, tenure, remuneration, and superannuation."

It is, however, clear that the power to act on these decisions is to a greater or lesser extent limited by the ability of the council to take action. As was pointed out in the last section this ultimately depends on Cabinet assent. Since some items have been the subject of statutory action, it is not possible to modify them without considerable intra-governmental bargaining. One such matter is the noncontributory superannuation scheme established by act of Parliament, dating back to the last century. There is no superannuation fund and the amount required to pay the benefits has to be voted annually by Parliament. The civil servant has no "right" to benefits. The principles of the scheme are discussed in Whitley subcommittee; individual grievances are taken up outside of Whitley. Such discussions are much more by way of consultation than those over, say, remuneration. However, no fewer than five amending Civil Service Superannuation Acts have been passed since World War II, and in each case the staff side participated in drafting its conditions. Once discussions upon matters covered by statute pass beyond the point of agreement and mutual recommendation to the Cabinet, then the staff association is of course free to pursue it through other channels such as parliamentary lobbying; as long as it remains on a joint committee agenda it is not usual to adopt this course.

The flexible manner in which these "exclusions" are interpreted reflects the manner in which discussions on practically every item of civil service administration are carried on. There is no clear distinction between negotiable items and items upon which consultation may take place. Formally, however, this is provided by the limits set upon arbitration for certain items (see *Dispute Settlement* below). The long-term plans of the Civil Service Department are discussed in detail and proposals put by staff side are carefully formulated in their own committees and generally given equal treatment with those of the government. Two recent examples may serve to illustrate this process. Dispersion of staff is a nonarbitrable item, but departmental proposals for the setting up of provincial computer centres involving the movement of tax officers from the London area were put to a meeting of IRSF delegates in 1966 after executive discussions, and the location of centres amended according to staff suggestions. On a more permanent basis subcommittees of National Whitley are set up on most long-term policy matters. A second example would be the present reorganisation of the service following the publication of the Lord Fulton Report on the Civil Service in 1968 which is taking place along the general lines suggested by a Joint Whitley Committee.

Despite this emphasis given to Joint Whitley Committees, negotiations on matters of remuneration or conditions affecting the members of any one of the individual staff associations can and are frequently taking place with the national and departmental representatives of that association. This is particularly true of negotiations which set the level of each individual grade, as against the general percentage increases in the overall amount of salaries and wages negotiated.

A most important procedural point within collective bargaining is the use of the tentative and nonbinding offer. For example, this enables the offerer to make sure that the offer is accepted in the terms in which it was made and not misinterpreted and used against him. It does, however, denote an element of trust since it conveys the commitment of the offerer to that particular form of final bargain. The nonbinding or "without prejudice" offer is used extensively in Whitley and individual association (in-grade) negotiations particularly within the hard core of arbitrable subjects including emoluments (current earnings), hours of work, and annual leave. Such offers may on occasion be passed outside the Whitley framework to membership for informal soundings, but usually they are retained within the documentation passing between the secretariats of the two sides. The "without prejudice" conveyance of information is particularly important in the statistically complex system of "fair comparisons" used in pay negotiations.

As in other parts of the British system, the process of union "ratification" of any negotiations before an agreement is made is unusual within the National Whitley or in-grade discussions. Outside of constant reporting back to their executive committees (at least once a month) association representatives face their most important test when, as part of the executive who carry responsibility for the completed agreement, they present a resolution of ex post facto approval of the agreement. Special meetings of members have on occasion been called during the course of important negotiations (as in the inland revenue case mentioned above) but these are usually for the purposes of "tension management" in relation to the strategic conduct of negotiations. In small departments and within single offices two way communication in the course of local negotiations is much greater, but at this level most business consists of individual grievances.

The individual grievance procedure is not well coded except to the extent that such grievances should not normally find their way onto Whitley agendas unless as the basis for a more general claim or issue. Behind this rather negative approach lies a reality very similar to that in private industry by which the individual may take his grievance to his branch or office representative after raising it with his supervisor. After local discussion between the local union representative the issue must go straight to departmental level. In reality this means contacting the national officer of the staff association who is usually located at national headquarters. He can then raise the matter with the Establishments Division of the department. If the aggrieved member can get no satisfaction at this level there is normally nothing more to be done. In the processing of grievances it may be discussed by the lay committees at various levels of the staff association who may press the issue as one with more general implications; in this case it can enter the Whitley machinery as a general issue. Much depends on the quality of service and advice offered by unpaid union officials to the individual member, because all civil service (and Post Office) unions have highly centralised professional resources, not readily available to provincial members.

All agreements upon substantive issues reached by Whitley Committees have to be promulgated as Treasury circulars or minutes. Hence with few exceptions Estacode constitutes a whole series of Whitley decisions covering all aspects of pay and conditions of service. Not all decisions in Estacode are Whitley decisions, however, many of them being taken unilaterally either without staff side requesting consultation, or having been consulted have disagreed without wishing to go to arbitration. Whitley decisions are contained in the staff side Whitley Council bulletin circularised monthly to staff representatives at all levels.

In common with British practice these agreements are often both ad hoc and open-ended, that is any single issue can be reopened and, with the consent of the other side, can be re-negotiated at any time. However, since 1955 there have been two important developments towards a formal, regularised and closed-end agreement. This has consisted of two parallel movements, one towards regular reviews of salary levels in each grade treated separately, the other towards all-service increases over an agreed period of more than a year.

PAY RESEARCH

The basic problem in pay determination in the civil service and in other areas of public service in which no price is put on the product of labour is to determine what is "fair." That is to say fair to the employee in that it is a competitive rate, whilst being acceptable to the taxpayer. During the early years of unionisation civil service rates were usually higher than those in comparative employment and union protest concerned the introduction of cheaper labour in the form of women and boy clerks. The development of the concept of the determination of salary levels in the civil service by reference to "fair" comparisons with those in outside employment stemmed from a commission report of 1923 which ultimately resulted in a cut in service salaries. In 1931 the Tomlin Commission considered that "Civil Service remuneration should reflect what might be described as the long term trend, both in wage levels and in the economic condition of the country."[5]

In fact the prewar position of the civil servant was such that the formula was not put under severe test until the late 1940s. By 1950 the real salary level of clerical officers had declined by 21 percent over 1932, that of administrative officers by 43 percent. These losses compared with a general wage rate that had gone up by 8 percent. In 1949 the CPSA submitted a claim based on long-term trends which was rejected because of the economic condition of the country. Subsequently

5. Royal Commission on the Civil Service, 1930-31, Final Report, para. 308.

the SCS commissioned a private agency to conduct a survey of earnings in outside employment, to which the Treasury replied with one of its own. Finally, it was decided to set up another commission.

This Royal Commission (Priestley Commission) presented its report in November 1955. Besides proposing new scales of pay for most of the main categories of the civil service the report had the following to say on the principles which should govern pay:

1. The end to be served by principles of pay in the civil service may be stated as the maintenance of a civil service recognised as efficient and staffed by members whose remuneration and conditions of service are thought fair both by themselves and by the community they serve.

2. The primary principle of civil service pay should be fair comparison with the current remuneration of outside staffs employed on broadly comparable work, taking account of differences in other conditions of service.

3. Internal relativities should be used as a supplement to the principle of fair comparison in settling civil service rates in detail, and may have to be the first consideration when outside comparisons cannot be made, but they should never be allowed to override the primary principle or to become rigid.

4. In applying the principle of fair comparison a clear distinction should be made between fact-finding (that is the two processes of establishing job comparability and the discovery of the pay and conditions of service attaching to jobs regarded as comparable) and negotiation.

5. Fact-finding should be assigned to a branch of the civil service not directly connected with those divisions of the Treasury responsible for questions of pay and conditions of service.

6. Means should be found of enabling the staff associations to participate fully in fact-finding.

7. Fact-finding should be a continuous and detailed study carried out at first hand by qualified and experienced staffs, and in the first process involved, namely establishing job comparability, they should keep themselves informed of developing techniques in the field of work comparison.

8. In the second process of fact-finding, namely the collection of information on pay and conditions, the fact-finding unit should confine itself to assembling and listing strictly factual material.

The report of the Royal Commission was considered by the Civil Service National Whitley Council. In a joint statement issued in April 1956, the Council agreed that "fair comparison" was a valid and valuable principle in civil service pay negotiations and announced their intention to establish a fact-finding unit in accordance with the recommendations of the Royal Commission. It was to be known as the Civil Service Pay Research Unit (PRU), to be under the general control and direction of a committee of the Civil Service National Whitley Council (since come to be known as the Steering Committee) and to be under the day-to-day control of a director appointed by the Prime Minister. The staff of the unit was to be provided by civil servants of appropriate grades posted to it for periods not normally shorter than three years.

The method to be used in comparing the facts about pay and conditions were described by the Royal Commission in this way:

> We consider that the Civil Service should be a good employer in the sense that while it should not be among those who offer the highest rates of remuneration, it should be among those who pay somewhat above the average. Expressing the point in statistical terms we should say that if it were possible to obtain for any specific job a set of rates "representative of the community as a whole" which could be arranged in order from top to bottom, . . . the Civil Service rate should be not lower than the median but not above the upper quartile.

> In practice, however, the selection will rarely, if ever, be representative of the community as a whole since we have proposed that it should consist of "good employers." This, so far as it goes, leads us to suggest that the right range within which to make comparisons should be around the median. It will, however, be clear from what we have said in the earlier part of this Section that the process of settling

rates is not a simple matter of comparing money rates of pay inside and outside the Service. On the contrary, it involves a number of stages. First the outside rates have to be adjusted, rate by rate, to take account of what are quantifiable, if not always precisely quantifiable, factors; rates so quantified we term "true money rates." . . .

If a collection of true money rates can be ascertained, it is still not possible to arrive at more than a "provisional" Civil Service rate until account has been taken of the unquantifiable factors. . . .

At this stage there may often be room for doubt and we think that the Civil Service rate should be given the benefit of any such doubt so that in practice the Civil Service adjusted rate will tend to lie above rather than below the median of the outside true money rates.

While both the provisional and the adjusted rates will sometimes be related to a particular point on a Civil Service scale (minimum, maximum, or an age-point), it may very often only be possible to obtain a span within which the scale should lie.

In current practice this process involves four main stages. In the first a selection of outside employers is made who may, and usually do, include other public service establishments outside the civil service. A selection of civil service jobs within the grade under review is also made. This selection involves negotiations between staff associations and the Civil Service Department in which neither side can veto the suggestions of the other but a strict limit is placed on the number of firms and internal jobs to be surveyed by the PRU. Secondly the work study and collection of data on earnings and working conditions is carried out by the PRU and submitted to the staff association and to the Civil Service Department. The firms' names are excluded from the reports at this stage. The research departments of the two sides then take over the data and both work out true money rates for each outside comparison (analogue) and median and upper quartile rates. Simultaneously the job descriptions are examined by a joint working party.

Irreconcilable differences in interpretation are left open for the final negotiating stage in which the general secretary of the staff association or his deputy meets representatives of the Civil Service Department of similar status.

The PRU began its work in 1957 and evolved a schedule designed to bring about settlement for all of the main grades, once every five years. Most of the departmental and many of the specialist grades became "linked" to the former and received increases in line with them. The examination of job descriptions and the calculation of true money rates became fruitful subjects for bargaining long before the final stage of the process had been reached. In 1963 it was agreed to reduce the descriptive data and to accept some uniform interpretations of the true money rates. By this means the cycle over which each grade was examined was reduced to four years. In 1970 this cycle was further reduced to two years. The continued reduction reflects both the growing impatience of members with the length of time taken before perceived injustices can be "rectified," and also the increased ability on the part of negotiators to reach an understanding on perennial sources for disagreement, e.g. the value of the civil service noncontributory superannuation scheme when compared with contributory schemes in outside industry.

THE LONG-TERM AGREEMENT

In addition to the principle of "fair comparisons," the Priestley Commission of 1955 also recommended that "In times of unusually marked and rapid movements in outside rates the pay of the lower and middle ranks of the service should be adjusted by means of a central settlement based on a single formula, which will be a matter for negotiation in the light of evidence available about trends in comparable outside employment. . . ." It became increasingly clear that the overall rate of increases in pay during the 1960s was such that central agreements should be normative practice. Between 1957 and 1963 all-service increases were negotiated each year except 1959.

In 1960 an agreement was made within the Whitley Council which allowed for a review to take place if in November of any year the cost of living index had risen by five or more points over the period subsequent to the last settlement. The official side also undertook to maintain internal relativities and to allow increases in exceptional circumstances. Before the agreement was formally ratified by staff side it was submitted by each association to its annual delegate conference (convention). It was rejected by the conferences of several major associations and was therefore not ratified. Official side proceeded as though it had been ratified and gained the general cooperation of staff side in working it, up to the imposition of the government's general "pay pause" in August 1961.

On that date the Chancellor, Mr. Selwyn Lloyd, announced that no further increases could be considered and that in the proceedings before the Civil Service Arbitration Tribunal the operative date of any award would not be arbitrable. Later in December, a national staff side claim was submitted on the basis of rise in the general wages index. A substantial increase was meanwhile allowed to workers in electricity supply on the grounds of productivity gains. This increase emphasised the deprivation felt by other public service workers and the CPSA announced a work-to-rule to start in February 1962. The Chancellor announced immediately that the "pause" and the constraints on arbitration would end on April 1, 1962. Concurrently the Treasury made an offer of a 2 percent increase to staff side who responded by submitting their claim to arbitration. In June they received an award of 4 percent back dated to April 1.

This fracas is presented here as one explanation for the greater willingness with which the 1964 pay agreement was reached and agreed by civil service associations. This agreement not only confirmed the four-year cycle of research and reviews, but also offered guaranteed annual increases of 3 percent in the first year and 3.5 percent in 1965 and 1966. Such closed-end agreements were becoming increasingly prevalent in the public services and in private industry during 1962 and 1963. They were almost encouraged by the belief that no government would interfere with freely negotiated agreements of this kind. (The interference of the government in private arbitration agreements during 1961/62 had been condemned by representatives of the Ministry of Labour.)

But, perhaps as important, it was seen by staff association leaders as the beginning of a new "escalation strategy" in which every civil servant would be kept crudely aligned to increases in earnings outside the service but would receive a periodic in-grade audit. However this strategy was frustrated with all similar movements to closed-end agreements which took place in the early 1960s by the complete ban on automatic increases in earnings during the 1966-67 period. The last instalment of the all-service increase was never made although delayed increases gained through PRU exercises were allowed. In May 1968 the Chancellor informed national staff side that a ceiling of 3.5 percent would be placed on increases in civil service salaries as on those outside. Because of the loss of the last increase in the long-term agreement a total increase of 7 percent would be allowed to civil servants in 1968 to be made up of all awards in respect to PRU in-service or all service claims. Anything above the 7 percent would not be paid as an increase until January 1969. There followed a general all-service settlement of 3.5–5 percent in June 1969 and a further ad hoc settlement averaging 8.5 percent in February 1970. All of these were supplemented by in-service raises through PRU. In addition a totally unusual aspect of a separate general claim made in June 1968 was for an increase to all earning less than £15 per week. This emphasis was followed in the 1970 agreement in which an aggregate minimum of 10s was placed on the award.

The latter emphasis was common to all unions following TUC policy in 1969 and emphasises the degree to which staff associations find an affinity with the wider movement in times of stress, particularly under incomes policy. On these occasions public employees are of course particularly exposed. It seems however that a unique civil service pay strategy emphasising the use of job-comparisons in maintaining relativities but providing a general escalator clause covering all grades, has for the time being suffered a major set-back.

PAY IN THE HIGHER CIVIL SERVICE

On the recommendation of the Priestley Commission a Standing Advisory Committee on Pay in the Higher Civil Service came into existence in February 1957. It undertakes periodic reviews of the pay of grades above that of principal (i.e. the initial career grade in the administrative class) and covers all civil servants with major administrative or policy-making responsibility. Its reviews may be undertaken on its own initiative or at the government's request. In either case it acts as an independent body, reaches its conclusions independently of government as employer, and submits its recommendations directly to the Prime Minister. Its recommendations have direct effect on nearly 1,200 members of the administrative class but through linkages with professional and other grades some 8,000 civil servants are covered in all by its awards.

In 1965 its third report was referred to the NBPI under the terms of the discriminatory powers of the Minister for Economic Affairs contained within the then existing incomes policy. The Board reported very quickly within two months and found the SAC's award to be justified under the criteria of incomes policy. However a furor arose out of the Minister's statement that "fair comparisons" was no longer to be regarded as sufficient reason for pay increases within the civil service. In July 1969 the government accepted an SAC recommendation that senior grades should receive increases of 11–12 percent. These were considered to be within the "norm" because of the four-year gap since the last award. The increases of £1,200 per annum for permanent secretaries and proportionate awards made to other grades made considerable impact on tax-paying workers whose incomes were themselves under restraint. When the SAC came forward eight months later with the suggestion of increases of up to 43 percent the government felt constrained to award only half of the suggested figure. On April 15, 1970, more than 300 senior civil servants held a protest meeting and the leader of the IPCS threatened difficulties in the negotiations then taking place on the organisational restructuring of the service.

DISPUTE SETTLEMENT

Disagreements cannot be resolved within the Whitley machinery by majorities made up of staff side members over official side or coalitions: though in fact in the British manner a consensus without quantitative assessment is possible over many issues. If neither will make concessions a "failure to agree" is recorded. Unless a request for reference to arbitration is made, the will of the government prevails and is put into force by what is variously described as "administrative" or "executive" action. It would be unwise to discount the importance of this executive power in the make up of estacode; for in much of the rule-making process the great difference between the private and public sectors lies in the quality and length of time spent in prior consultation. On matters controlled directly by Acts of Parliament such as superannuation this is certainly so, as is this case with the granting or refusal of established status to individual employees.

There is a further aspect to the constraints on the scope of collective bargaining. In private industry the boundaries of "management prerogatives" have been pushed back by the ability of employees to assert sanctions. In the civil service, as is common in Australia, disputes of interest, as well as of rights, are arbitrable and both parties have agreed to use arbitration as the last stage of the procedure. In the absence of other sanctions reference to arbitration has taken on a significance unlike that anywhere else in the British system. It denotes a breakdown in the highly valued trust between the sides. The unwillingness of civil service management to allow certain subjects to go to arbitration may indicate its sensitivity to outside criticism on these matters. In the Whitley agreements these exclusions extend to all matters pertaining to manpower planning—numbers and complements of staff, grading arrangements, promotion, mobility, together with scheduling of hours within the weekly total (shift work), classification of work, and even to the physical conditions of work. Furthermore insofar as the Whitley Committee Agenda act as individual grievance procedures they do not end in outside arbitration, for no matters concerning individuals can be submitted to arbitration. These issues are all regarded "as matters of management in which the employer must have the last word."[6] At a time of considerable change in the structure of the service these constraints to the powers of the staff side to go to arbitration may be particularly important.

They are manifested in the conditions under which one party may impose arbitration on the other as part of agreed procedure. According to the Civil Service Arbitration Agreement of 1925 (incorporating subsequent modifications) either party can take a claim to arbitration by a body of permanent umpires comprising the Civil Service Arbitration Tribunal. This tribunal can deal with the claims which affect emoluments (a term which includes pay allowances, overtime rates, subsistence, and travelling and lodging allowances), weekly hours of work, and scales of annual leave. These are of course major substantive issues and decisions to go to arbitration are not taken lightly by either side. There is in fact a gentleman's agreement that staff side as a whole will not use arbitration in normal circumstances. Nor is it a general practice for any of the major staff associations catering for general grades to use arbitration: all but three cases in the last six years have been raised by the Institution of Professional Civil Servants, the Post Office Engineering Union, and the Inland Revenue Staff Federation. The departmental or special grade status of these associations reflect the fact that all of the cases taken to arbitration had to do with the earnings of grades whose salaries were not contained in mainstream negotiations and who were concerned with their differential status.

For the many small staff associations not directly represented, or not represented at all, on Whitley Councils, arbitration is also a means of expressing their continuing grievance. This is particularly so for "breakaways" like the Guild of Telephonists who attempt in this way to prove their worth over the parent organisation. Since the introduction of the pay research exercises associations representing linked grades have also had far more

6. H.M. Treasury, *Staff Relations in the Civil Service,* London, HMSO, 1965 para. 80, p. 21.

information upon which to dispute Treasury offers. This possibly accounted for some of the newcomers to arbitration during the 1950s, but in general the decline in the use of arbitration since that time has been most marked. In 1951 the number of disputes taken to arbitration was thirty-eight; in 1961 eighteen; in 1969 only three cases went to the Tribunal.

The 1969 figure may be accounted for in the effects of government incomes policy. Staff side associations have grown increasingly distrustful of the degree to which "the public interest" intervenes in arbitration decisions. Even if this were not so the threat of NBPI intervention *after* the process of arbitration is a sufficient deterrent to prolong negotiations. In some recent cases departmental staff sides have requested that a claim be submitted to arbitration, as mentioned previously. Generally the decline in arbitration probably stems from the growing confidence shown by association representatives (though not always by members) in the process of pay research. This process supplemented by all-grade claims make arbitration awards which deviate from the trend more difficult to obtain. In addition such claims often mark a desire on the part of the supplicant to depart from the overall level of increases obtained by others on the staff side. In a more hostile economic climate staff side is displaying a greater degree of solidarity.

The procedure is that when one side registers a "failure to agree" the Ministry of Labour must be informed of the desire of that side to go to arbitration. Usually the consent of the other side enables a joint approach to be made. The minister refers the issue to the Arbitration Tribunal consisting of a permanent independent chairman appointed by the minister with two others, one of whom has been drawn from a panel of official side nominees and the other from a similar panel of staff side nominees. Both of these panels are ministerial appointments but nominations come from the respective sides of the National Whitley Council. They may be renominated every two years; only civil servants and officers of civil service unions are excluded. Most are in fact academics and in 1968 Professor H. A. Clegg, a former member of the staff side panel, was appointed chairman.

In the case of "fringe departments" (those offering direct service to commerce) such as the Atomic Energy Authority, it is usual to set up an ad hoc Tribunal under the Industrial Court Act 1919 consisting of persons chosen from the panels of the Civil Service Arbitration Tribunal. The traditional method is adopted in respect to hearings. Fifteen days before the issue is heard, parties to the reference have to supply copies of their case to the Tribunal who sends each a copy of the other's statement. The statement contains all submissions upon which the party relies in presenting his claim. Until 1968 the statements were read at the hearing and all evidence, oral or written, is related to the latter. A synopsis of the statements was published with the final award of the Tribunal, but no attempt was made to explain the basis upon which the award was made. In that year the new chairman introduced a new procedure whereby statements had no longer to be read, but a presentation could be made in a manner which brought out only the salient points. More important however was the change in the presentation of the cases. The Tribunal gave the reasons for their awards where they thought it desirable to do so; their presentation was in fact extremely limited and did not attempt to draw on any previous body of knowledge. Nevertheless this change was welcomed by many staff associations and indeed by official side representatives. In the past some awards had been known to create unworkable anomalies which could not easily be put right by a return to the same anonymous process by which they had been created. On the other hand increased information laid the arbitrators more open to the charge of being influenced by incomes policy.

The terms under which the Civil Service Arbitration Tribunal operates have been changed by unilateral decision of the government on two occasions. The first, between August 1961 and April 1962, suspended its powers to determine when awards would be put into effect. This suspension and its renewal under the Prices and Incomes Acts of 1966, 1967, and 1968 was a specific and short term measure to ensure the maintenance of the incomes norm for increases throughout the labour market. In the latter acts the norm was specified and anything above it became subject to delay under the general terms of the acts. Both suspensions produced immediate protests: public demonstrations were organised on the first occasion and after the second most of the major staff added strike procedures to their rule books.

THE EFFECT OF THE ABSENCE OF MEDIATION

Since the abolition of the Civil Service Arbitration Boards in 1922 there has been no place for mediation or conciliation in Whitley procedures. These have been considered to be outside of the spirit of Whitleyism by the official side; not all staff associations accept this interpretation and some gave evidence to that effect to the Royal Commission on Trades Unions and Employers Associations (Donovan) 1968. Attempts have been made by civil service and post office unions to employ the services of Ministry of Labour (now DEP) conciliation officers but these have been consistently refused by the minister of the time. The CSCA evidence to the Royal Commission (page 13) suggested "that there well may be room for some form of standing conciliation machinery—particularly on matters which do not proceed via the Whitley Councils" channels of negotiating—which could, before a final state of disagreement, bring the views of independent persons to bear. As things stand today, if agreement cannot be reached on a nonarbitrable item, the only courses of continued action open to the union are those of pressure, e.g. public campaigning, parliamentary campaigning or some form of "direct action."

By such action, the unions are going beyond a simple demand for mediation or conciliation, and are in effect criticizing the narrow range of arbitrable items on the Whitley agenda. Even before these limits are reached it is clear that discussions can often end in deadlock without either party wishing, for its own strategic reasons, to go to arbitration. On many issues, particularly nonarbitrable issues such as grading or complementing, public and parliamentary sympathy cannot be counted on or the issue is too complex for presentation in this manner. Most usually such issues occur at departmental level and they can become perennial sores which underlie complaints or day to day grievances. Clearly the present judicial form of arbitration in which evidence is presented and the "solution" discovered on the basis of formally restricted presentations of the case makes arbitration of limited value in many such situations. Nor can awards be easily made and accepted on matters of management organisation or politically sensitive subjects like civil service complementing. A case for mediation on a wider range of issues is easier to make and might be an antidote for a detectable feeling among staff associations that they are locked into a relationship which inhibits their taking effective action on behalf of their members in some fields. For management such an institution might dispose of constantly recurring grievances.

THE RIGHT TO STRIKE

Civil servants are not subject to any special prohibitions on the withdrawal of their labour. Every individual civil servant has the same right to leave his employment after serving notice of his intention to do so upon his employer. Indeed as Crown servants they have no procedural contract and can walk out any time without that step rendering them actionable at law. However a strike is of course no more than a temporary withdrawal of labour designed to improve, not to terminate the long-term content of the employment contract. In this respect the civil servant is probably more exposed to disciplinary action on the part of his employer than other employees. In moving the 1946 Trades Disputes and Trades Unions Bill the Attorney General said "I take the opportunity of making it quite clear that this government, like any government as an employer would feel itself perfectly free to take any disciplinary action that a strike situation that might develop demanded."

The position of the "Crown servant" is such that he can be dismissed at any time. However the dependency of the civil servant upon his employer stems not so much from the nature of his contract as the basis upon which his noncontributory superannuation payments are made by his employer. Continuity of payments into the fund are imperative for pension benefits to remain at the prescribed level; breaks in payment of less than a year may be counted as a full year's absence and prolonged breaks can lead to loss of all previous credits. This disciplinary deterrent was most often quoted by staff side representatives in their role as leaders at annual union conventions up to recent times.

Until 1964, strike action had been confined to one or two day stoppages, usually of a spontaneous and unofficial kind. In the Post Office there had been a number of occasions when staff worked to rule or barred overtime. In 1961 members of the CSCA threatened a "work to rule" as a protest against the government's interference in arbitration procedure but unfettered arbitration was restored before the threat was implemented. Apart from the possibility of disciplinary action no civil service union maintained a strike fund and the low level of subscription paid by the members simply did not allow such a strategy to be contemplated on an official basis. Of course in private industry most strikes were unofficial. Generally however unofficial and unconstitutional actions are not part of the public servants' armoury. The importance of procedural conformity and of being assured of the legitimacy of his actions by his representatives has always been important to him. The commitment of the leadership to the Whitley machinery has always, therefore, provided an important constraint in times of stress. The change of mood in the 1960s has probably been as much determined by leadership strategy as by growing tension among members. In other words the role of general secretary is much closer to the American leadership function of "tension management" than is generally the case in British industry. The decision taken by the CSCA convention in 1969 and of the SCS convention in 1970 to set up internal procedures for beginning and ending strikes and for paying strike benefits mark an important extension to the armoury of their leaders. Both executives gained the power to transfer funds to temporary strike funds: in the previous year the manipulative grades in the CSU had set up a permanent strike fund.

The first major strike was in fact in the Post Office in

1964 over a long-standing pay grievance dating back to the 1961 pay-pause. It was a general one-day action called by the Union of Post Office Workers and was followed by more long drawn-out unofficial strikes by many UPW members. Since that time strike threats have been made by several civil service unions, but the largest and most prolonged series of strikes were called by the CPSA among its members in the newly formed Post Office Corporation between January and March 1970. These did not directly test the power of the civil servant to strike but they certainly appear to have set a tone for future action by SPSA members. In fact the right of a civil servant to strike has been tested on several occasions in unofficial with-drawals among industrial and Post Office grades dating back to the middle of the last century. In such disputes any disciplinary action taken by the official side against strike leaders has usually been supported by the staff associations concerned. Such action has as recently as 1968 included the suspension or dismissal of civil servants in the Post Office.

It is perhaps significant that the introduction of strike activity coincides with the widespread loss of faith in arbitration as representing an independent view.

LOBBYING: THE USE OF THE PARLIAMENTARY PRESSURE GROUP

In general, lobbying is confined to the actions of individual unions. That is to say that the national staff side have deliberately refrained from adopting pressure group tactics as a normal method of procedure for fear of prejudicing the long term ne-gotiating relationship with the official side. This has not pre-vented individual associations from organising extremely effec-tive lobbies on a regular basis, nor indeed from co-operating outside of the official machinery of the staff side secretariat. Two issues will serve as examples, superannuation and equal pay. Both are "exempted" subjects in the sense that they cannot enter into Whitley discussions, leaving staff associations little choice but to go to the source of decisions in Parliament if Whitley discussions are ineffective.

Staff side has lobbied Parliament whenever unfavourable changes in the superannuation scheme are likely to be affected. In 1970 the Minister for Social Security brought forward a state scheme which implied a contributory element in the civil service scheme. Staff Side canvassed M.P.s on this issue. More important is the regular campaign launched every few years when the level of pensions paid to civil servant pensioners is reviewed in the House. The most important public campaign was that for equal pay between the sexes. Throughout this century pressure has been brought by staff side upon Parliament resulting in House of Commons resolutions in 1920, 1936, 1944, and finally 1952. The latter led to a nation-wide petition organised in 1954 in cooperation with the National Union of Teachers, NALGO (Local Government) and the National Federation of Professional Workers (a loose federation of clerical unions). After promising discussions in his budget speech, the Chancellor initiated discussions within Whitley, Burnham, and in local government. It was agreed that equal pay should be introduced by instalments over a seven-year period.

At the present time only two Post Office unions and those representing industrial civil servants maintain political funds, i.e., funds registered as being retained for political purposes and therefore maintained from special membership contributions. This has been so since 1948 when the CPSA ended an association with its former general secretary who for eight years had set in the House as their parliamentary general secretary. Before that, this M.P., Mr. W. J. Brown, had been a founder member and first full-time officer of the CPSA (then CSCA) after which he was supported as a Labour M.P. by voluntarily collected funds between 1929 and 1931. During his period in Parliament he was probably more effective in pursuit of CSCA ends than most union M.P.s but he was also an individualist who eventually took up an anti-TUC position in the House. In 1947 the CSCA executive proposed to end their contract with ·Mr. Brown, an act which he took before the Committee of Privileges of the House. He failed to establish a breach of privilege but in the resolution put by the Prime Minister, endorsing the Committee's decision, the House condemned all contracts with outside bodies which in any way stipulated that M.P.s should act as their representatives. When Brown resigned from the CSCA in the following year a phase in staff association development ended and, outside of the Post Office, no attempt at such representation has since been made by civil servants.

THE INDUSTRIAL CIVIL SERVANT

These total approximately one half those of the nonindustrial service and are employed in the manufacturing and maintenance sectors which are responsible to ministers of state in a more direct manner than in the case of public corporations. That is to say that their accounts are subject to the estimates and supply procedures of the House of Commons, and are not covered by the self-financing provisions of the 1961 white paper (see Section II) and other statutes applying to public corporations. They are most concentrated in the Ministry of Defence where their numbers have been growing in an inverse relationship to the rundown in military personnel; the Ministry of Works where they include construction workers responsible for major building works as well as maintenance workers on ancient monuments; H.M. Stationery Office, one of the largest printing houses in the U.K.; and the Royal Mint.

Their status as Crown servants is similar to that of nonindustrial civil servants. After an average probationary period of two years they are considered for certification as established civil servants and entrance to the superannuation scheme. In practice only about 50 percent of industrial civil servants are established and as vacancies occur within establishments "temporary" staff are given the opportunity to become established in order of seniority. The rights and responsibilities of established staff are similar to those of the "manipulative" grades of the nonindustrial civil service. The benefits in terms of pay and working conditions are rather different since they are determined by reference to those applying outside industrial employment, though following those in the nonindustrial civil service in respect to sick pay and superannuation.

Industrial civil servants receive the same written encouragement to join trade unions as that given to nonindustrials and union representatives in government employ are entitled to the same facilities in respect to their union duties as those afforded to staff associations. Most industrial civil servants were not restricted in their union membership by Section V of the Trade Disputes and Trade Unions Act 1927 because at that time the majority were unestablished. As a general rule industrial employees now belong to trade unions which are not confined to the civil or even the public service. The largest numbers are members of TGWU and the GMWU (see Section II) but among the noncraft workers organised by these general unions the density of unionisation is not high, possibly no more than 30 percent. In addition to these main unions, a range of craft unions are recognised at national and/or departmental level, the largest being the Amalgamated Union of Engineering Workers; the Electrical, Electronic Telecommunication Union; the Society of Graphical and Allied Trades; the Amalgamated Union of Building Trade Workers and the Amalgamated Society of Woodworkers. Among the groups covered by these unions, the proportion of membership is much higher but they comprise no more than 25,000 employees or 11 percent of the whole.

The principles, structure, and content of the negotiating machinery in the industrial sector are also different to that in the nonindustrial and to some extent reflect the differences in union membership. During 1919 and 1920 steps were taken to apply the principles of Whitleyism to government industrial establishments. This was done by a scheme agreed with the unions for a number of joint councils. The councils were of two kinds, Trade Joint Councils and Departmental Joint Councils.

There are three Trade Joint Councils, each representing trades or occupations which were most representative of civil service industrial work in 1920—the Engineering Trades Joint Council, the Shipbuilding Trades Joint Council (in effect Navy Section, Ministry of Defence), and the Miscellaneous Trades Joint Council. The councils consist of one side representative of the ministers of the departments, together with the Civil Service Department, Treasury, and DEP, the other of the unions representing workers in the trade. These employees are located over a number of establishments and are directly employed in a number of departments. For that reason seven Department Joint Councils exist in the major employing sections or departments. Councils have not been set up for departments with small industrial staffs; in these cases there is direct negotiation with the trade unions concerned.

The Trade, Joint Councils (TJCs) deal with questions of wages and other conditions of service which may be applied nationally and in relation to those pertaining within any trade outside the service. Departmental Joint Councils (DJCs) act in a similar manner to those in the nonindustrial civil service in respect to the interpretation and application of TJC decisions and work arrangements within each department. They also have powers to set up local machinery in plants within departments for the purpose of local negotiations and consultation within management. Added to these three levels is a fourth, that of the Joint Coordinating Committee for Government Industrial Establishments which deals with conditions common to all industrial civil servants for example, sick pay, superannuation, and holiday pay. The allocation of seats on the official side of this committee is similar to that of the TJC but the union side is composed of three representatives of each of the TJCs.

Other than this latter provision the size of the councils may vary according to the wishes of the two sides within the particular trades or departments; there need be no equality between the sides. The allocation of seats is determined by each side but representatives have to be officially endorsed (or supported) by the minister for a probationary period of one year. With the permission of the council, representatives of a constituent body other than the appointed representative may attend either as a substitute or in a consultative capacity; persons with special knowledge of a trade may also be co-opted. Formally therefore the constitution of the TJCs and DJCs is less rigid than that of the Whitley machinery in the nonindustrial sector. This holds to the extent that the employees' vice-chairman presides at meetings in the absence of the official side's chairman, or in the absence of both he can be chosen from either side.

Though the TJC schedule of quarterly meetings is usually maintained more rigorously than on the National Whitley Council a great deal of business concerning particular sections is carried out in subcommittees composed of representatives of management or the trade unions concerned. New items of business come before councils either by agreement between the joint secretaries or when raised under "any other business." Once a question has been included on the agenda it remains until both sides agree to remove it. This usually occurs after agreement on action has been reached or disagreement recorded.

The scope of bargaining is however somewhat different from that in Whitley. The objects of the Trade Joint Councils as set out in the Constitution are to "secure by means of regular joint discussion . . . the fullest measure of cooperation in the settlement of questions relating solely to the trade so far as it concerns employees in that trade." The substantive issues to be settled are enumerated as the "regular consideration of the rates of wages of persons in the trade . . . together with readjustments as may be necessary, subject to due consideration being given to such national or other agreements as may be fixed for the trade from time to time." Other questions include hours, holidays, conditions of entry into the various establishments, "and training therein in the trade."

Managerial considerations like the collection of data on output, costing etc., are included in the objects of the JTCs but it is clear that at the trade level the primary concern of the craft unions who dominated the discussions leading to the formation of the JTCs was that their members should not be paid less than the going craft rate or accept inferior conditions of work. From the official side the underlying principle on which the rates of pay of industrial civil servants is based derives from the Fair Wages Resolution of the House of Commons. The original resolution dates from 1891 but the form of words was passed in 1946. It refers only to government contractors and requires them to pay rates of wages and observe hours and conditions of work not less favourable than those observed by the appropriate trade or industry in the district in which the work is carried out or by employers in similar circumstances.

In 1910 the government undertook to apply the same terms to its own employees and for many years after the establishment of the JTCs each government establishment fixed its own rates in accordance with an average of the rates paid by other employers in its district. By 1940 national wage rates had displaced local wage rates in most outside industries and it was only then that the two sides agreed that rates were to be negotiated and applied from the national level. Since then a highly centralised system has been developed for determining national rates of pay by alignment with the average of the national rates paid in a selected number of outside industries. The pay structure is in two parts, one for craftsmen and one for noncraftsmen.

The basis for the craft rate is the average of the minimum time rates paid in a selected group of industries (a separate sample being taken for London). To this are added supplementary payments based on skill and experience measured on a scale designed to bring earnings up to time work earnings in industry. Noncraftsmen are divided into unskilled, whose earnings are based on an average of the agreed minimum time rate in selected industries (four geographically different samples), and semiskilled workers who receive a "lead rate" on the unskilled rate. The size of the lead is again calculated by reference to the extra amount paid above the unskilled labourers' rate. The craft and unskilled rates are calculated at six monthly intervals by reference to the average movement in rates in the selected industries, and adjusted from April 1 and October 10 in each year. Lead rates and supplementary payments have been renegotiated at much longer intervals of up to four years. Women in the industrial civil service were not covered by the Equal Pay Act of 1957 and like most of their sex in private employment are paid at 85 percent of the men's rate. Payment by results schemes common to a large proportion of engineering and manufacturing in the U.K. cover only about 15 percent of the industrial civil service.

The net result of these arrangements is that government workers figure among the lowest paid manual workers in the country; 13 percent were below a £15 per week "subsistence level" in December 1969. There are wide differences with government employment between the minority on incentives, schemes or working regular overtime and the many unskilled workers who have their pay fixed in relation to national wage rates but not national levels of earnings. Differentials within the wage structures have been eroded by the built-in lag between increases in the basic and the supplementary or "lead" payments. Labour turnover is high in many establishments and often over half of the employees are above the age of 50.

In a situation in which the market position of employees is so poor, the consultative spirit of Whitleyism is hardly likely to be present within local committees. There has, however, been very little attempt on the part of Treasury to make a national injection of the esprit de corps which is commonly ascribed to the nonindustrial civil service in Whitley publications. More tangibly the former Treasury Management (Services) Division which was, and now within the CSD is, responsible for promoting the use of up-to-date management techniques by departments has been almost wholly concerned with the nonindustrial civil service. More lately, under threat of NBPI Report No. 18 (1966) on the pay of industrial civil servants, the Treasury set up a standing interdepartmental committee "to promote continuing improvement in efficiency in government industrial establishments." This action in itself implied that the use made of existing procedures had been totally inadequate.

On the Board's recommendations pay agreements have recently been signed on a departmental basis and provision has been made in such arrangements for plant-level bargaining on changes in working practices in exchange for higher earnings. But the longer term objectives of the Board included the integration of industrial civil servants with nonindustrial, on the basis of salaried employment similar to that already existing in the Post Office. Already some former "industrial" posts had at that time been elevated in status under market pressures but objections had come from the existing union representatives who feared loss of their membership to civil service staff associations.

The Board's recommendation for integration was couched in strong terms. It suggested that the division of employees into "staff" and "workers" was outdated and that as author of the incomes policy the government ought to set its own house in order before recommending "staff" or "salaried" status for manual workers as a means to bringing about the abolition in government of restrictive practices common in private employment. It added that the existing external unions should take a full part in negotiating these changes in status and should be accepted thereafter as the representatives of "manual" staff within an integrated civil service. There has not been any acknowledgement of this part of the report by either side of the existing Whitley machinery.

SOURCES OF CHANGE: THE EFFECT OF THE FULTON PROPOSALS AND OTHER TRENDS

The proposals for changes in the structure of the civil service are potentially the most important factor acting to bring about changes in the nature and content of collective bargaining in the civil service. The present system of between-class promotion is based on the most general needs of the service in both qualitative and quantitative terms. Appraisal boards are untrained. Upward mobility is extremely limited and horizontal movements between the professional, scientific, or technician grades into senior administrative posts are still exceptional. Job evaluation does not go beyond the broad amorphous definitions of the general classes.

The structure of the staff associations reflects these barriers to mobility and in fact they have historically allied themselves with the Treasury in creating the vast heterogeneous main classes. Their motive was the classical union attempt to bring about a common minimum rate set at the highest quality of work contained within the grade. Attached to these main grades are the many minor Treasury and departmental grades representing the inability of any central authority to impose an exacting scheme of job evaluation upon the service. Each provides a means to whip-sawing or leap-frogging in the separate pay negotiations which take place for each grade. In particular the action of the Post Office in detaching itself from staff side in most general claims, and of the Institute of Professional Civil Servants in pursuing the defence of its members' differentials to arbitration on more occasions than any other staff association, shows their sense of separateness and their distrust of the administrative class of the civil service who sat opposite them across the negotiating table. The grievances felt by the professional, scientific, and higher technical classes should not be minimised. Numbers in these classes have grown from 37,687 in 1947 to 78,516 in 1966. The feelings of deprivation often expressed by professional scientists working in industry are focussed and intensified by the formal and very manifest obstacles to their lateral movement into the civil service career streams which would lead them to the most senior positions. Not only are their frustrations qualitatively greater, but their numbers are also far more significant than those of any similar group brought together by a common employer in the U.K.

The Fulton Committee criticised three main aspects of the civil service structure. Most important was the complexity and multiplicity of classes, but this was of special importance because class barriers made it impossible to develop staff. Combined with these structural rigidities was a shallowness in the competence of administrative and executive officers. It suggested that some attempt should be made to group jobs into those providing an administrative career structure and those amenable to task specialisation. At all times the task content of the post should be considered first and an attempt be made to fit the man to the job through appropriate aptitude and appraisal procedures. At senior levels the scientific and professional class should give way to the concept of occupational groups allowing free lateral movement into and out of the present administrative class. Class barriers between the executive and administrative classes should be abolished in order to allow a career in either administrative or specialist occupations to be followed by those showing particular merit within their job.

A start has been made with an interim merger between the executive and administrative grades, designed to go further in 1971 subject to approval of the proposals by the conferences of the staff associations involved. A review of the work of the clerical classes has been conducted and discussions are taking place with the staff associations with a view to restructuring the work of these grades. Clearly these changes *could* have immense implications for the future structure of the staff associations themselves. But in the short run they can be set against the trend in the government's policy in the wider field of industrial relations. In particular the work of the NBPI on negotiations in the public services has constantly emphasised the need for bargaining which is specific to the needs of the immediate work unit. In this way it appeared to them, as to the authors of the Donovan Report, that pay increases could truly reflect increases in productivity.

The change of government has, if anything, increased the likelihood of greater attempts at cost control in Whitehall. The introduction of a team of business consultants as permanent additions to the new CSD has coincided with attempts to impose "output-budgeting" upon the purchasing departments of the Treasury. It is not unlikely that any widespread job-evaluation exercises entered into would bring about a return to departmental or occupational specialisms. These would enable local productivity increments based on skill or merit to be offered by managements, a move which would almost certainly be resisted by staff associations whose caution in approaching the Fulton proposals is already evident. Even if such local agreements do not become usual, it seems probable that the demands upon the centrally based nuclei of full-time officers employed by staff associations is going to increase. Any great movement towards professionalism in office or departmental personnel management will tax the ability of this relatively small number of union leaders to deal with the application of specialist managerial techniques at local level.

This movement of negotiating activity outwards from the center has already been evident in the post-War period. Many large groups of staff dealing with specialist functions have now been physically removed from the proximity of Whitehall by the government policy of dispersal of civil service functions and staff to the provinces, particularly to the "development areas" in the north of England and Scotland. Whereas before the war two thirds of the civil service lived and worked in London, now precisely the reverse ratio applies, with the larger proportion working long distances from London. The result has been reflected in the larger amount of work undertaken by voluntary branch-level officers. But in addition there has been a change in the staff recruited and, in the character of association members. In urban centres entrance standards have been relaxed or bypassed through internal promotion. In the provinces large numbers of ex-industrial workers have been recruited to the lower grades. At the same time the process of negotiation has become more "scientific," certainly more professional, than the ritualistic and sometimes charismatic leadership processes usual with bargaining outside the service. From 1957 onwards dissidents at every annual staff association convention have presented motions attacking pay research. Their arguments are perfectly rational ones: the exercise of "fair comparison" *has* a built-in lag which *has* tended to keep public service pay—not just civil service pay—behind that in the private sector. Staff association leaders beset by criticisms by NBPI have to fend off attacks from those who wish to return to completely ad hoc bargaining in which arguments are based on rises in the cost of living. Support for these arguments is widespread and difficult to handle because the process of pay research is so entirely anonymous and cut off from the membership. With the perversity of the "generalist" civil servant, staff association leaders have tended to emphasise the exactness and "scientific" nature of the relatively crude statistics and job analysis involved in the process. This isolation has been another source of membership frustration.

Under the stress caused by incomes restraints and the overriding of arbitration procedures, there has been a growing tendency for staff association members to demonstrate their feelings in public demonstrations. So far the leaders of the staff associations concerned have been able to channel these feelings and these actions into support for strategies undertaken within the Whitley machinery. It may be that if issues become more localised as a result of the Fulton proposals, such national strategies will prove to be insufficient.

While changes in the nonindustrial civil service cannot be related in any way with trends in the industrial civil service, it seems possible that in a period of increasing militancy among public service manual workers elsewhere that they too may become more inclined to adopt a militant posture. Very much depends upon the ability of the Whitley structure to adapt to these changes. This ability ultimately rests in the capacity of the principal actors at national level to recognise the changes and respond to them in an appropriate manner. For some time at least one should expect staff association leaders to be more concerned with manifesting the frustrations and protest of their members than in restoring the atmosphere of Whitleyism. In doing so they may well be preserving in a paradoxical manner the machinery which they have temporarily been forced to neglect.

·IV·

Industrial Relations in the Post Office

POSTAL and communications services have provided one of the major trading activities of the government since the sixteenth century. In 1931 the Tomlin Commission found that the Post Office employed just over half the existing civil servants. At the time of its gaining financial independence as a separate public corporation in October 1969 its labour force was still almost two thirds that of the rest of civil service taken together despite the postwar expansion in other government activity. Throughout its history a considerable proportion of Crown servants have been postal employees and it has tended to be the most innovative in the creation of new forms of employment. During the nineteenth century the introduction of cheap postage brought an expansion of the postman labour force. In 1869 the inland telegraph service was nationalised, and in 1912 the telephone service was taken over completely (with the exception of a single small city). These changes brought large numbers of technical and manipulative staff into the civil service. The Post Office also operates a banking service, set up in 1861, and it has subsequently become an agency for other government services, such as the payment of old age pensions. These in their turn have brought into being large concentrations of office and counter clerks.

The present-day activities of the Post Office are carried out under four divisional heads: postal services, telecommunications, the National Data Processing Service, and the Savings Bank and Giro. Of these the NDPS represents a new commercial venture designed to offer on-line computer facilities to any outside customer. Giro is a recently introduced bankers' order system working outside of the national clearing banks and is regarded by them as a potential rival. Both of the latter are innovations as is the newly granted power given to the Post Office to manufacture its own equipment. While these changes have a direct bearing on the present trends in industrial relations, any study of the Post Office must focus upon two sections of employment, the postal services and telecommunications. It is within these areas that the organisation achieved an early monopoly and in which the occupational groups have attained their most distinctive separate identities.

The breakdown in employment on September 30, 1969, appears in Table 3.

Table 3.

Post Office Employment, September 30, 1969

Staff Group	Total Staff
Administration	
Headquarters and regional Headquarters	20,333
Savings and Remittances	
Giro	2,815
Savings departments	14,328
Postal Field Staff	
Post Offices (mostly counter clerks)	33,706
Mail operations (postmen)	125,802
Engineering (most internal)	3,357
Telecommunications	
Operating staff (switchboard, telegraphists, etc.)	61,620
General and engineering (engineers, linesmen, labourers)	140,689
National Data Processing	1,797
Purchasing and Supply	8,898
Motor Transport	6,532
Total	419,877

Note: In addition 22,662 Subpostmasters are employed on a subcontracting basis and are paid on a scale of fees. 31,000 part-time staff are counted as half.

Source: Public Relations Department, Post Office Corporation Headquarters.

THE CHANGE TO PUBLIC CORPORATION STATUS

Up to 1933 the Post Office was run like any other government department. Since then there has been a series of changes, culminating in the Post Office Act of 1961. Between 1961 and 1969 the finances of the Post Office were entirely separate from those of the rest of the government and were reported to Parliament by commercial accounts only. These accounts related to a Post Office fund under the management and control of the Postmaster General. Like public corporations, it had to ensure that its revenues covered its costs "taking one year with another," though this meant that unprofitable services such as the telegraphic service were subsidised by others. Investment could be financed by advances from the consolidated fund through the Exchequer or by temporary loans from the Bank of England subject to a target for return on capital of 8 percent in the manner set out in the 1961 white paper, "The Financial and Economic Obligations of the Nationalised Industries" (Cmnd. 1337, April 1961). The staff nevertheless retained their status as civil servants, and the Postmaster General was a member of the government, answerable to Parliament for the activities of his department in the same manner as other ministers.

In 1967 the Postmaster General announced that the Post Office was to become a public corporation responsible in Parliament to a Minister of Posts and Telecommunications. General powers for the operation of the corporation were vested in a chairman appointed by the minister and a board of directors, with statutory limits of between three and twenty-six. Nine members were in fact appointed, six from private industry together with Sir Richard Hayward, former Secretary General of the Civil Service Whitley staff side who became industrial relations director with overall responsibility for relations with employees. These directors took over their responsibilities from October 1, 1969.[1]

From that date onwards the minister's responsibility for the day-to-day operations of the Post Office gave way to one of maintaining a general oversight of the performance of the corporation with respect to its statutory responsibilities, both social and economic, and to maintaining the £2,800,000,000 limit on monies borrowed from whatever source (consolidated fund, Bank of England, and approved outside sources). Most important is the ministerial duty to prepare the annual accounts of the corporation in a manner approved by the Treasury and to present them to the Comptroller and Auditor General, before laying them before Parliament. Thus in effect once a year

1. Post Office Act 1969, Eliz. 2. Ch. 48.

the minister becomes responsible before Parliament for the activities of the Post Office. In practice the chairmen of the other major public corporations operating under similar checks have worked very closely with their ministers in the planning of long-term investment. The basic political strength of the minister is the power to appoint or dismiss the directors, but it is one that has rarely been overtly used. Both he and the chairman have however to submit to the scrutiny of the House of Commons Select Committee on Nationalised Industries which has the special function of examining the reports and accounts of the Nationalised Industries and other Boards whose main source of finance include the Exchequer.

While the work of the latter body is largely concerned with establishing suitable criteria for investment and expenditure, pricing and servicing policies are subject to the scrutiny of consumer councils. In the Post Office case this council is known as the Post Office Users Council and together with three country councils has advisory powers with respect to the minister. There are numerous examples of the disregard in which these bodies are held by directors of public corporations. The more important price criteria used by public corporations arise out of targets for returns on net assets set by the minister under the provisions of the 1961 white paper. Almost all price increases in publicly owned services are justified in these terms or in terms of the needs of the internal funding of investment. In the quasi-corporative role which the Post Office adopted in 1961 it has been subject to these criteria for nearly a decade with a visible effect on the state of its industrial relations.

THE STATUS OF THE POST OFFICE EMPLOYEE

Before 1969 the Post Office employee was a Crown servant and was subject to the same restricting responsibilities and benefits as civil servants in other departments. The fact that a majority of Post Office employees were in "manipulative" or "industrial" grades gave them considerably more freedom in respect to the political aspects of their trade union activity than was generally the case within the civil service. The latent disciplinary constraints upon strike activity including the loss of superannuation "rights" were more applicable in the Post Office than in the rest of the "industrial" civil service because the majority of the higher grades of industrial and manipulative staff were established officers. Indeed while differences in substantive conditions between grades were considerable, within the departmental Whitley machinery as in all other internal departmental procedures, differences in class or grade were not generally recognised.

On the vesting day for the new corporation Post Office employees ceased to be civil servants. They were employed in exactly the same manner as any other employees save that the government gave an assurance to Post Office unions that their terms and conditions of work would not suffer in any way by dint of the transfer. This has in fact been established as being so in subsequent negotiations, and although Post Office employees become subject to all of the universally applicable statutory provisions for minimum periods of notice, working conditions, etc., their current individual contract of employment is very much superior to that provided for in such laws. The single major change, at the insistence of the unions, is to a contributory pension scheme in which the individual member can transfer the total employer/employee contributions to other defined schemes upon his movement to employment outside the Post Office.

The work of telegraphists still comes under the supervision of district postmasters, as does that of postal clerks in Crown post offices. The predominance of the local postal service has been an influence in structuring union organisation and the negotiating machinery for grades which might otherwise have gained separate representation. The majority of Post Offices offering counter service to the public are conducted however on an agency basis in private shops by people who have never been established civil servants. These subpostmasters are represented by their own association within the Whitley machinery but the subcontractual nature of remuneration is subject to a separate bargaining process between the Post Office and this association.

THE WHITLEY STRUCTURE

The Special History of Development in the Post Office

Basically the same machinery existed for the purposes of negotiation, consultation, and arbitration in the Post Office up to 1969 as existed elsewhere in the civil service.

Of the twenty-five members of the civil service national staff side ten were purely Post Office representatives together with the chairman. Six of these came from the Union of Post Office Workers, two from the Post Office Engineering Union. Of the remaining two, one represented first line supervisors in the Post Office, the other a loose federation of higher grade staff associations. Most of the general grade staff associations also had members in the Post Office, the greater numbers being in the (then) Civil Service Clerical Association whose membership was highly concentrated in the savings bank and Giro.

The superiority in numbers of the Post Office group when they acted together was such as to override any other sectional interest on staff side. However because of the measure of autonomy enjoyed by the Post Office unions to negotiate special conditions for its members in their Departmental Whitley Councils, this power was rarely used to press sectional interests. Yet by the same token it is fair to say that the involvement of the Post Office in the operation of the National Whitley Council was possibly less than that of other civil service departments. Postal unions were among the initiators of Whitleyism and had provided many staff side chairmen from the first appointment to the last as well as members of the permanent secretariat. Nevertheless the main weight of the negotiating effort of Post Office unions was concentrated upon substantive items arising within the departmental councils.

This emphasis in staff side effort stemmed from a number of factors, most immediately from the fact that only one of the twenty-four national official side representatives was from the Post Office. The issues arising within the department were influenced by factors outside of those affecting the rest of the service. The disparity between the department's importance and its managerial representation on the official side appeared to demonstrate an attempt to delegate decisions to an appropriate level. The budgeting position of the Post Office has always been related to an element of market pricing: the first combination of postmen in 1855 arose out of an economy drive when it was found that the penny post was not making sufficient profit. The technology of the department was also quite different from that elsewhere in the service. Little in the content of national decisions could be applied without considerable interpretation and most of the Post Office functions were quite outside of the experience of Treasury negotiators. That did not prevent the Treasury from asserting some external control over official side offers at departmental level but the experience of departmental official side negotiators was much more specific to the Post Office than was commonly the case in other departments.

In addition to these factors the Post Office unions themselves often chose bargaining strategies which involved the tactical use of general all-service increases when and if they were sufficient to act as an escalator for their members, without prejudice to their ability to negotiate separately on behalf of the grades they represented. This was of course the two-pronged negotiating strategy adopted by all civil service unions, most particularly departmental associations, but in the Post Office case it tended to demonstrate the entirely separate industrial basis upon which the department could gain pay increases related to physical productivity. This strategy was combined with a greater aggression in pressing their claims than that common among other civil service unions. The first strike by civil service unions was made by the associations of postmen and telegraph and telephone clerks in 1913 in pursuit of a wage rise.

The Departmental Councils

The Post Office differed from the rest of the civil service in having two Whitley Councils at departmental level, the one for industrial and technical grades known as the Engineering, Factories, and Supplies Departmental Whitley Council, the other for manipulative and clerical grades generally referred to as the Postal Departmental Whitley Council (nonengineers). The formal constitution of both committees did not greatly differ from that of other service departments. In the Engineering Council, the Post Office Engineering Union held half the staff side seats, in the Postal Council a majority was held by the Union of Post Office Workers. The official sides consisted of the Director General of the Post Office together with his appropriate chief sectional officers, the director acting as chairman of both councils. Like other departmental councils, their functions were those of negotiating changes in working conditions which were specific to the employees of the Post Office and of consulting over a wide range of nonarbitrable items of departmental policy. Differences between negotiation and consultation were often blurred and difficult to distinguish.

In practice the conduct of business was markedly different to that found in other councils in a number of important respects. Meeting of the Departmental Council took place regularly at six monthly intervals, and every three months the departmental staff side would meet to discuss a review of the financial performance and prospects of the department submitted to them by the Director General. Consultation was therefore on a much more regularised basis than elsewhere in the civil service. As long ago as 1929 a special staff-management committee was set up to discuss technological and organisational changes and both of the major post office unions have placed great emphasis upon educating their members to understand to accept changes in terms defined by their representatives.

The degree of consultation and even negotiation on organisational change was (and under the new corporation remains) quite considerable within both the regional tier of Post Office Whitleyism (such regional councils being unique to the Post Office) and within the 200 or so local councils at postal district and telephone area level. It is remarkable for two reasons. The first is that throughout its existence the Post Office has been submitted to quasi-commercial performance criteria which have perhaps a more positive feedback than the Parliamentary procedures normally applied within the general civil service. The second is that the technical complexity and the range of the substantive content of issues is often greater than that facing negotiations in the nonindustrial civil service. Technological change is likely to involve changes in the task content of the industrial (largely engineering) grades in the Post Office more than those of the manipulative grades. But even the tasks of postmen and mail sorters are generally more directly affected by the introduction of automatic scanning and sorting of mail than are those of the average civil service clerk by the introduction of computers. Less directly such technical changes as these have also affected the promotion prospects and career lines of many grades, particularly telegraphists and to some extent telephonists.

Long before the move towards a separate telecommunications line of command within the managerial structure of the Post Office, the unions had gained separate negotiating and consultation machinery for the main telecommunications engineering grades. The Engineering, Factories, and Supplies Council has served as a focus for much of the consultation and negotiation over the installation and maintenance of new capital equipment. The largest participant in such discussions has been the Post Office Engineering Union whose 90,000 membership is largely to be found among junior technicians and linesmen. This council was in essence the industrial grade body but the technical content of its agenda was clearly fundamental to changes taking place throughout the telecommunications sector, and, with the increasing automation of mail sorting, was determining the content of business in the Postal Council.

Of this latter body the Union of Post Office Workers predominated. Its 180,000 membership covers not only the 126,000 manipulative workers in the postal and sorting grades, but also the majority of telegraphists, telephonists, and the counter clerks (known as postal and telegram officers). Many of the strictly technical issues affecting the careers of postal employees were, then, dealt with outside of the Postal Departmental Whitley Committee as such. For some white-collar telecommunications employees working under the line supervision of postmasters and organised by a union in which postmen predominated, their situation has not always appeared totally satisfactory. The creation of a separate telecommunications command structure in the new Post Office corporation has intensified efforts by breakaway groups to parallel this in the union and bargaining structure.

Grievance Procedure and Discipline

Grievance procedure remains similar to that in existence in the civil service. Grievances may be advanced through joint-union procedures only if and when they have generalisable implications. Individual employees can appeal to various levels of management up to regional level and ultimately to the Director General if they wish. Previously they could appeal to the minister in Parliament, the Postmaster General, but in practice this was a rarely used right. All serious disciplinary offences require a written charge by the Post Office against the employee, who has an opportunity to reply. Dismissals can only be made by regional directors. Within three days of exhausting his own rights of individual appeal the employee may renew his appeal through the national union, notice of appeal by the union being given within a fortnight of rejection of the individual appeal. Union appeals are infrequent; the Post Office Engineering Union receives twelve appeals a year at headquarters and supports about eight. Most grievances are dealt with fairly speedily at local level without resort to either individual or the official intervention of the national union in the way set out above. A telephone call or informal meeting between management and union representatives decides the matter or makes it clear that there is nothing to be gained by going into official procedure.

The Structure and Character of Staff Side

In all some twenty-two staff associations were recognised at departmental level and most were represented either directly or indirectly on the Departmental Whitley Council; half of them had less than a thousand members. The multiplicity of organisations was attributable to the existence of a large number of higher grade groups who valued their professional identity. This independent identity was reinforced by the special conditions pertaining to the largely autonomous commercial sales and con-

117

tracts work of the Post Office. The continued existence of these associations obviously depended upon their effectiveness. This was achieved through the liberal approach of the Post Office in recognising all such associations if they considered them to be representative whether they had a majority of the appropriate group in membership or not.

Membership of the Whitley Council had also guaranteed the longevity of some smaller associations which existed in 1920. These would otherwise almost certainly have disappeared in the 1920s and 1930s when the membership of most civil service unions declined by as much as 30 percent.

The department's attitude has not always been seen as liberal by the unions. In 1946 the Postmaster General (Lord Listowel) announced that for the future recognition would only be granted within the department to associations that could demonstrate a 40 percent membership within the grade for which it was seeking recognition. It would be reviewed after a period of three years and if membership had fallen below 33.3 percent, recognition would be withdrawn. Four years later another Postmaster General (Mr. Ness Edwards) rejected this arithmetical formula, returning to the more traditional civil service view that recognition should "take into account wider questions, such as the effect of a change in representation on the general working relationships in the Post Office" (Hansard, May 17, 1950). This change in view created considerable dissatisfaction among some small and breakaway movements who had been running recruiting campaigns designed to bring them the necessary 40 percent membership in the grades they wished to represent. Their protests led to the setting up of a committee of inquiry in 1952 which set out three principles upon which the department based its recognition policy up to 1969. These were: (1) It is undesirable to have more than one union representing the same grade or group of grades; (2) the association claiming recognition should be required to prove to the Postmaster General's satisfaction that the existing recognised association has failed and was unable to look after the interests of the grades concerned; (3) the claiming body must be financially stable and so organised that it can serve its members better than the existing recognised association.[2]

Clearly these principles were directed at dealing with the problem of the small and unstable breakaway organisation and as was to be proved later, provided little guide to jurisdictional disputes between established unions. A precedent was recently set by the UPW and Civil Service Union when they used the mediating offices of the TUC in concluding a "spheres of influence" agreement in regard to radio-telegraphers.

As in the rest of the civil service, recognition by the Post Office management merely implied the right to be consulted on matters specific to the grade or grades for which recognition had been granted. The right to participate in the Whitley machinery remained to the departmental staff side to grant or to withhold. The development of two large unions, the Union of Post Office Workers and the Post Office Engineering Union, devoted to the principle of industrial or vertical unionism within their respective sectors of the Post Office has been accompanied by quite serious interunion disputes and breakaway movements. The Union of Post Office Workers has competed with a breakaway movement of telephonists for over forty years, and the continued existence of this organisation known as the National Guild of Telephonists owed much to its early recognition by the official side. The UPW was in fact formed in 1920 by the amalgamation of the long-established Postmen's Federation (1891), the Fawcett Association (of mail sorters), and the Postal Telegraph Clerks Association (1881) together with the telephonists. The latter groups have from time to time thrown up dissidents demanding greater attention to their special status and earnings differentials. In particular post and telegraph officers have been concerned to maintain their status relative to that of savings bank clerks. These latter jobs were graded as civil service clerical officers: it was in the savings bank that the organisation that was to become the Civil and Public Service Clerical Association was formed in 1903. The result of this

2. Report of the Post Office (Departmental Classes) Recognition Committee (Lord Terrington), February 1952, Cmnd. 8472.

separate organisation has been to promote considerable tension between the UPW, which was trying to retain the allegiance of the post and telegraph clerks, and CPSA, which was attempting to retain the superior market position of its clerical members.

The POEU has also been beset by breakaway movements. Although craft demarcation was abolished in the Post Office under a remarkable agreement made between management and the unions in 1911, its place has been taken by a grading structure requiring telecommunications training and certification. Breakaways of the more qualified engineers took place in the 1920s and between 1945 and 1953 the union competed with a similar dissident group of senior technicians. Associations like that of the Society of Telecommunications Administrative and Controlling Officers remained in existence with a membership of 76 up to the formation of the new corporation. Yet the splits represented vertical functional divisions as well as status differences. The National Guild of Motor Engineers, a breakaway among the Post Office truck servicing mechanics, was quite successful until the Armitage Report brought an end to the efforts of most such minority movements in 1953.

As a result of these splits the UPW and POEU have developed internal occupational or trade sections with national officers specialising in each group. Separate conferences and separately elected representative committees also exist within their constitutions; both types of gathering have only limited power and the national executive committees in whom final authority rests, tend to be dominated by postmen in one instance, and junior technicians in the other. In the POEU the full-time officers are appointed by the executive, still an unusual practice in Britain, where the election of national negotiating officers by the whole membership, as in the UPW, is more usual. Since 1936 the POEU have specified that the new appointee to General Secretaryship "should be a man of about 30 years of age, with an education of university standard, and must belong to and be imbued by the aspirations of the working class."

In part of the fervour with which the UPW and POEU approach both the concept of Whitleyism and the need for an industrial structure for their unions stems from the ideology of guild socialism or workers' control over their own sector of industry. This ideology is written into the constitutions of many British unions formed during large amalgamations which took place in the period 1913 to 1925. In the case of these two unions the tradition has been kept alive by Whitleyism which has often been cited in the speeches of union leaders as an example of worker participation in management. Of the two organisations the UPW has been most identified with this view but both unions were early affiliates to the TUC and to the Labour Party. After the repeal of the 1927 Trade Disputes Act, which prevented all organisational affiliations outside of the civil service for a period of twenty-one years, they both rejoined the TUC. The POEU did not, however, resume its affiliation to the Labour party until 1964 after what it described as a "period of disturbed relations between the Post Office and the union." Clearly the ideological attachments of these unions have become somewhat instrumental in character. They nevertheless remain very important influences within the workings of the TUC and the Labour Party. The general secretary of the UPW is assured of a permanent place on the TUC General Council; the present general secretary of the POEU is an active Labour politician and was made a life peer by the last administration.

THE SPECIAL PROBLEMS OF FINANCE

The Post Office is one of the biggest trading organisations in the U.K. with a surplus on current income of almost £128 million in 1968/69. In the same year total *new* investment amounted to over £40 million. It is also one of the largest and most labour intensive of commercial employees, 75 percent of postal costs being direct labour costs. Principal among the reasons for the increased separation of functions under departmental heads from 1967 onwards was the desire to achieve greater precision in performance and investment criteria. The need for increased economic accuracy was emphasised by the Select Committee on Nationalised Industries Report of that year which condemned the overall target figure of 8 percent per annum return on capital previously set for all Post Office services. As a result of its recommendations differential targets were set. The labour intensive and economically static postal service was given a target of only 2 percent on total expenditure; the rapidly expanding telecommunications branch was set a return of 8.5 percent on net assets, later raised to 10 percent. All of these changes were preliminary to the ultimate financial independence gained by the Post Office. The Committee's view that the inland telegram service, with a deficit of nearly 43 percent, should be treated as a noncommercial activity was not acted upon.

Confusion as to whether the Post Office should or should not be treated as a "social service" was reflected in the price tariff which failed to reflect either the differences or the continuous changes in the quantitative demand for a number of services during the 1960s. Within the attainment of the overall profit target there was considerable nonsubsidisation between services. Much of it was unintentional; the return on postal services in fact rarely rose above 28 percent, though up to 1968 its performance was judged against the overall 8 percent only attained in aggregate through the contribution of the Telecommunications sector. Direct services provided for the government, in particular the provision of counter services to the national savings scheme, payment of pensioners, and receipt of license fees, etc., were all charged at cost with no attempt at profit. In such an ambiguous decision-making environment a great deal of emphasis was placed upon restraining postal labour costs rather than upon investing in labour-saving equipment.

The introduction of mechanical mail sorting and automated telephone exchanges was slow. Although it was never officially suggested, the opinion that protracted consultation slowed the rate of new investment was widespread among Post Office management. Against this opinion can be set the fact that market forecasts vastly underestimated both the number of new households to which mail had to be separately delivered and the number of households demanding a telephone for the first time. With little flexibility in possible price changes and only modest investment plans the department at first turned an intransigent face to staff side pay claims. As a result staff wastage rates grew especially in postal services and overtime working increased to 26 percent in some regions. During the 1961 pay-pause the unions withdrew their cooperation from the joint production committees designed to increase efficiency by purely voluntary means. It was against this background that the first productivity bargaining was initiated in engineering, factories, and supplies departments in 1964 and that a major modification to civil service pay research procedures for postmen and mail sorters was introduced in the same year.

The Post Office now hopes that its new financial freedom will enable more flexibility in pricing policies and hence in pay agreements. It has already resulted in increased postal and telephone charges. Much of the financial benefit derived from the former was almost immediately passed on in a pay increase for postmen. It remains to be seen whether the ultimate financial check on pay claims will be located in actions taken by the management side of the new corporation or by the Minister for Post and Telecommunications. It has even been suggested that the loss of personal esteem felt by postmen in their dealings with the public will check future pay claims. It seems at least as likely that such discord between the public and the Post Office will act as a stimulant to more militant bargaining. Already the accent has shifted from the time-consuming processes of joint consultation to productivity bargaining in which the union sets a price upon the cooperation offered by its members to employers, and in which management expects a smooth and speedy implementation of technical and organisational change. Such bargaining would hardly have been possible on a national scale without the existence of the comprehensive machinery for negotiation and consultation at all levels inherited by the new corporation.

THE SCOPE OF BARGAINING

The content of bargaining and consultation within the department is to be found codified in the collection of departmental circulars in which agreements, arbitration awards, and managerial decisions were propagated. This collection is known as Post-acode and formerly supplemented the Treasury rules contained in Estacode. When the Post Office corporation was set up it was agreed by management and unions to continue to operate these rules subject to changes required by the change in employee status and to modifications made by overtime. It was envisaged that these modifications would completely replace the original documents as new rules were created to meet changed circumstances. Indeed many of the management suggestions for changes in job grading and other matters had been discussed with the unions for two years prior to the change to corporate status in anticipation of this event.

The agreements made within the Departmental Whitley Council and in negotiations between management and separate unions were generally speaking open-ended ones. Up to the last general pay raise given to the civil service before separation, the UPW and other unions representing manipulative and clerical executive grades took advantage of most all-service claims made by national staff side. Unions representing engineering, factories, and supplies grades rarely did so, as the POEU is particularly insistent on separate negotiations for the grades it represents. The reasons for this are to be found in the nature of the work and in their desire to maintain the differentials of their higher grade members both within the corporation and vis-à-vis groups of technicians in the private sector.

Fundamentally important modifications in telecommunications equipment led management to suggest a productivity deal covering engineering staff in which a number of changes were made in working practice in order to reduce overmanning and to allow greater flexibility of labour between tasks. The first of these agreements was made in 1964, giving annual pay raises over the next three years to engineering grades, raises which were substantially above those gained elsewhere in the service. This initiative was followed some two years later in the manipulative and clerical grades where further changes in work practice and redeployment of staff were obtained by management in exchange for pay increases. Unlike the first, most of these subsequent agreements have been one-time deals offering a single pay raise or improved benefits in exchange for a specific employee undertaking rather than a three-year package. The reason for this was the union frustration experienced during the pay freeze of 1966-67 which cut off the last instalment due on long-term agreements. However, by the same token national incomes restraint, to which the only exceptions included productivity deals, served to precipitate much of the interest in such deals within the Post Office. In this respect Post Office unions and management reacted in quite a different manner from the rest of the civil service, a paradox which is explained by the differences in finance and technology described above.

In-grade settlements could, then, be obtained in three ways. General increases in pay and changes in conditions could be obtained through negotiations within the National and Departmental Whitley Councils. Gains could also be made by in-grade settlements negotiated separately by each union for particular groups of employees, especially more recently through productivity deals made this way. Apart from these two methods of gaining raises for their members Post Office staff side also supported and benefited from regular ingrade settlements.

Pay Research Exercises

Since 1957 these exercises carried out by the Civil Service Pay Research Unit have had a special significance in the Post Office. It was in fact a Post Office arbitration award which in 1927 first declared that the civil service pay should be set in terms of "fair relativities with outside industry." The interpretation of this principle (see Chapter VI) has been a constant source of controversy within the Post Office since 1956. In part this was due to the disappointment felt by both POEU and UPW members at the early pay research settlements. Both manipulative and technical grades had suffered an enormous setback over their prewar position vis-à-vis manual workers in private industry. Both had anticipated that pay research would re-establish their former differentials in the event it proved difficult to discover any groups of service workers or telecommunications engineers of sufficient similarity and numerical size to be described as analogous or "fair comparisons." The Priestley Commission had anticipated this difficulty in paragraph 664 of their report: "we think that any such comparisons may well have to be supplemented by more general comparison on the lines indicated by the Union of Post Office Workers (in testimony) namely by looking at skill, initiative and responsibility required for the work of these grades and for broadly similar tasks outside the Service."

By 1961 the worsening position of the postmen relative to that of outside manual workers and the government's decision to suspend both negotiation and arbitration during the national pay pause led to a four week work-to-rule which only ended with the retraction of government restraints. However, the postmen's claim for a raise was forced to arbitration where the UPW repeated their view that fair comparisons could only be made on the basis of a factorial job analysis based on a number of defined features abstracted from the multivarious task descriptions in the manner common in private industry. Since the Arbitration Tribunal refused to comment on this view the government, under threat of a strike, was persuaded to set up an independent inquiry. This body, the Armitage Committee on the Pay of Postmen, reported in June 1964. It found that the current sample frame, consisting solely of low-paid service industries, was the correct one from which to draw comparisons for the postman's job but that the method of comparison should be changed to that of job evaluation by factor analysis. In fact, the subsequent pay research exercise did not take place until after widespread unofficial strikes and a one day official stoppage followed by a work-to-rule and overtime ban throughout the country in July 1964. Job evaluation ultimately resulted in a pay increase to postmen of 13 percent which was regarded as an exceptionally large amount at that time.

At present there is little sign that any of the Post Office unions intend to initiate moves to carry on the use of pay research with or without job evaluation under the new corporation. Recent claims for overall increases for particular grades have been based on crude comparisons with national average earnings and cost of living indices made in the traditional manner. Concurrently local claims have been made on the basis of changes in work practices at plant level. It seems likely that so long as unions are prepared to place an emphasis on productivity-related increases in pay, management will not press for a return to "fair comparisons."

DISPUTE SETTLEMENT

Before the creation of the Postal corporation the Post Office operated under the Civil Service Arbitration Agreement 1925 which made arbitration compulsory on the application of either side, such applications being referred to the permanent Civil Service Arbitration Tribunal. The latter had no conciliation or mediation function and could only deal with claims which affect emoluments, weekly hours of work, and scales of annual leave. Successive governments had stood by the agreement to implement the Tribunal's awards "subject to the overriding authority of Parliament." Of the 607 cases arbitrated in the civil service between 1925 and 1959, 113 concerned the Post Office. Until 1950 the POEU had not itself made request for arbitration though it had complained on several occasions that the Post Office was failing to negotiate reasonably in order to avoid the responsibility for settling wage disputes. In the light of the ambiguity surrounding the financial goals of the department and the "cleft stick" in which departmental management were placed between strongly organised unions and the Treasury "mandarins," this union accusation seems an eminently logical one.

Shortly after Vesting Day (the day on which the new postal corporation was to come into being), an agreement was reached on the form and powers of the new Post Office Arbitration Tribunal. The Tribunal will consist of (1) an independent chairman nominated by the Secretary of State for Employment and Productivity; (2) one member drawn from a panel of persons constituted by the Secretary of State as representing the Post Office, i.e. nominees of the Post Office directors; (3) one member drawn from a panel of persons constituted through the same process but being nominees of the unions. In all cases appointments are to be made from persons outside the employment of the civil service, Post Office, or the unions in these sectors, and are to be considered for reappointment once every three years.

In default of settlement by negotiation of any matters relating to rates of pay or other forms of remuneration either party may require the other to support a joint application to the Secretary of State to refer the dispute to the Board of Arbitration. (This procedure is in accordance with that laid down in the Industrial Courts Act 1919.)

The procedure in respect to the presentation of the respective cases and in terms of the issues which may be dealt with are broadly similar to those existing in the civil service. Where on any reference the members of the Tribunal are unable to agree as to their award, the matter will be decided by the chairman.

Up to September 1970 no use had been made of the new procedures and indeed negotiations were still going on over the appointment of arbitrators. The spirit of the previous civil service agreement had been transgressed by strike action on only two occasions. On July 16, 1964, under considerable pressure from members who were already on unofficial strike in many sorting offices throughout the country, the Union of Post Office Workers called a national one-day strike in support of the postmen's pay claim. Though the union was in an extremely strong position it was clear that the leaders acted with some reluctance; on the second occasion the leaders' reluctance was even more marked. For seven months the union had negotiated for a pay rise for 3,500 overseas telegraph operator members to compensate them for anticipated losses in their earnings as a result of technical changes in working conditions. These operators came out on unofficial strike throughout December 1968 and picketed their central London offices. Even so the union took a ballot of its telegraph operators before calling the strike, and finally the general secretary made an unsuccessful appeal to the minister to appoint conciliators. On January 20 an eleven-day strike of operators began during which a complete ban on overtime and Sunday duty was operated by all post and telecommunications staff, in addition to a one-day strike which was imposed in nineteen key Post Offices. This strike received widespread public support and resulted in a public confession of error from the Postmaster General. In addition, however, it served to demonstrate to the minority group of telegraphers that they could call on the help of the much larger numbers of postmen in support of their claims, so long as they remained under the UPW umbrella.

In 1964 both of the major Post Office unions set up fighting funds in order to be able to take strike action in response to the intransigence which had been shown towards pay claims by their employers over the previous three years. Although they have threatened strike action on several occasions, the union leaders have been most reluctant to actually carry out their threats. At the 1970 conference (convention) of the UPW the unions' leaders reasserted their sole authority to call strikes and their policy of only using it to advance national rather than local claims. As centralised organisations containing groups of members the leaders of both the POEU and UPW are anxious to retain their ability to contain the strike sanction and to use it only as a last resort in their dealings with the new corporation.

CHANGES IN THE BARGAINING STRUCTURE UNDER THE NEW CORPORATION

The government's intention to transform the Post Office into an independent corporation was first announced in 1966. The major unions began their preparations immediately. Their preliminary aims included a rationalisation of the grading structure to eliminate a number of higher grade small groups enjoying preferred rates and to open the management structure to promotion from technical grades. Another was to recreate new Whitley machinery in a commercial environment and a third was to eliminate the plethora of small associations and the general civil service union representation on the new Whitley Council. In the pursuit of the latter aims the two major unions were prepared to withdraw their support from any new joint machinery in the corporation unless there was a reduction in numbers of representative bodies; a reduction which would of course benefit them by transfer of members. In pursuit of its total industrial union goal the UPW made advances to the POEU, but, not for the first time, the POEU replied to the effect that they regarded telecommunications as a separate "industry" from that of postal services.

In any event few major changes were made in grading structures or other working conditions along the lines suggested by the unions. The real changes came about in bargaining machinery. In August 1967 the two biggest unions were joined by the largest supervisory grade associations, the Society of Telecommunications Engineers and the Association of Controlling Officers in the formation of a council of Post Office unions (COPOU) representing some 320,000 of the 420,000 Post Office employees. The four unions drew up a scheme according to which all grades would be divided between them for the purposes of representation.

A year before Vesting Day this council set up a permanent secretariat modelled on that of the national Whitley staff side of the civil service. It had a secretary general and a national secretary for post and another for telecommunications. Progress in arranging the proposed "takeover" was slow, and the STE absorbed one similarly sized association catering for grades of an equivalent status. Ultimately it appeared that the 324 professional civil servants (IPCS) and 4,470 executive civil servants (STCS) might become merged with the two higher grade associations on the council, one of which (ACO) had changed its title to that of Post Office Management Staffs Association in order to facilitate the absorption of the three or four posmaster and higher management associations. For administrative grade civil servants the change in title did not appear to make the rose smell any sweeter, and for the clerical officer members of CPSA the move into their long-time rival organisation, the UPW, was also unacceptable.

The POEU came forward with a proposal designed to allay the fears of those associations who cited the long history of breakaways in the two major unions as reasons for retaining their small, closed, single status identity. It suggested that an independent board should be set up to arbitrate on matters concerning intraunion democracy. This suggestion, obviously modelled on similar machinery existing in the American United Automobile Workers union, would have provided an important precedent. At that time the more general Conservative Party proposals for a statutory body of investigation and individual court of appeal on all disputed internal trade union rulings was under active discussion; the TUC had counter-proposed that it should act in this capacity. Perhaps for this reason the POEU proposal was dropped.

Throughout this process the official side role was, to say the least, ambiguous; the confessed government mishandling of the overseas telegraphists strike served merely to increase the irritation of the postal unions. The minister, Mr. J. Stonehouse, had announced that the existing recognition of unions would not be changed until after Vesting Day and indicated that changes in union structure were matters for their concern alone. He did however express himself more positively in two regards. A month before Vesting Day the Society of Post Office Managers (SOPOM) came into being as a result of a merger of the four higher grade Post Office staff associations and members of the administrative and executive civil service associations (the latter having been previously committed to the Council of Post Office Unions). It is clear from a parliamentary statement (Hansard, November 11, 1968) and from other indications of support that the minister encouraged the formation of a separation association for senior management unattached to the council unions. It is also clear that members of former higher grade associations who took ballots on the proposal to form the Society of Post Office Managers expressed a desire to remain outside of the council by a vote of three to one. COPOU affiliates were nevertheless moved to complain to the TUC and to request political pressure be brought to bear on the minister. Finally the council threatened industrial action if SOPOM was recognised on Vesting Day and in fact corporation recognition was withheld until the latter's claims were modified to take in only higher executive grades and above.

Earlier in the negotiations a former minister had intervened in the merger process in order to facilitate the absorption of the Guild of Telephonists by the UPW. The guild represented only 18 percent of telephonists but it contained a large proportion of the male staff working on night shifts. They claimed that they would be inadequately represented by an industrial union in which telephonists were regarded as following a female or low status occupation and were therefore unable to maintain their shift differentials. The PMG asked a union nominee on the panel of civil service arbitrators to mediate between the two unions in a personal capacity.

As a result of these discussions the executive committees of the guild and UPW agreed to a transfer of engagements in early 1970 and the merger was put to a ballot of the guild membership as was required by the 1964 Trade Union Amalgamations Act. The members rejected the merger by a two-to-one vote. The management of the new corporation was requested by the UPW to withdraw recognition of the guild and complied by giving notice of their intention to do so on September 1970. The general secretary and the guild executive committee were forced to resign and the former was thereupon appointed to an organising post in the UPW.

In the interim the special structure of representation offered to telephonists as the price of guild absorption into the UPW organisation had added fuel to the resentment of telegraphist members of the UPW who had no separate voting or powers of delegation at national level. The union's disciplining of the leader of the unofficial strike of overseas telegraphists which had preceded the official strike of January 1969, led to the resignation of the local committee at the London head office of the overseas telegraph service. In July 1970 there was a delegate meeting of overseas telegraphists and international telephonists at which the formation of a Telecommunications Operative Union was announced. The new union can draw on the guild strength of 9,280 members together with that of overseas telegraphists. The industrial relations director of the corporation, Sir Richard Hayward, had previously already made it clear that such a union would not be recognised "in the foreseeable future."

It seems likely that the union will attempt to assert its independent identity during the foreseeable future and that whatever internal structural changes the UPW makes it will have difficulty in regaining the trust of these groups of employees.

The CPSA (the clerical civil service union) was faced with the loss of some 25,000 members on the formation of the corporation. Of its old Post Office membership 8,000 remained in the civil service since national savings were detached from Giro and the other commercial banking activities and retained under the wing of the Treasury. The rest became a prize for the UPW, a goal thwarted by the CPSA's refusal to join the council on terms which meant its eventual withdrawal in favour of the UPW. Instead it formed a separate posts and telecommunications group within the association and changed its name (the CPSA) to accommodate the extension in organisation outside of the civil service. The group was given considerable autonomy, much more than was enjoyed by the other civil service departmental sections within CPSA.

The CPSA received immediate recognition by the Post Office corporation, as did COPOU. Since however the council unions refused to enter joint negotiations with noncouncil associations, the CPSA entered its own productivity claim for clerical and executive officers. This claim signified two important changes in CPSA strategy. First, it had adopted the policy of selling out working practices in a manner avoided by all civil service unions. Second, it claimed that since the Society of Civil Servants had made an alliance with SOPOM its nonmanagerial members were unrepresented, so it commenced to recruit upwards into executive grades for the first time. In adopting this latter policy it clearly challenged the supervisory unions within the council.

Under pressure from the government to resist a claim which followed so quickly after a civil service central pay settlement, the Post Office refused to concede any claims until February 1970. By the new year the CPSA had set a deadline of January 19 on which it threatened a one-day strike, followed by the banning of certain duties, followed in February by "guerrilla strikes" in various parts of the country. The strike and work-to-rule had already taken place when a Post Office offer of much below what was offered to UPW members was received. Both the UPW and CPSA refused the offer at first and the latter body continued to refuse it after three weeks of half-day strikes and sudden walk-outs by its members. Finally the directors withdrew their offer and a local management locked out some half-day strikers when they returned to their office. This brought a mass walkout in London and Manchester, and the union extended its local strikes to one week periods. A settlement was agreed after two months during which most CPSA members in the Post Office had been on strike, though little money had been paid out of the union's strike fund. It had, however, proved to the corporation that it was as capable of taking effective industrial action as the much larger UPW. During the course of its strike the Post Office lost the much needed Giro, data processing, and telephone sales and was unable to capitalise upon its market penetration in these areas.

THE PRESENT STRUCTURE AND FUTURE TRENDS

At the present time the Post Office corporation has recognised and negotiated with three representative groups. The Council of Post Office Unions has expanded to cover nearly 35,000 employees represented by the UPW, the POEU, the Management Staff Association (formerly ACO), the Association of Post Office Executives (formerly STE), and the National Federation of Sub-Postmasters. The Society of Technical Civil Servants, the Institute of Professional Civil Servants, and the Telephone Contract Officers Association are represented pending the ultimate absorption of their members by other COPOU affiliates. In addition CPSA now not only covers clerical grades in the bank, headquarters Giro, DPS and elsewhere but has expanded to take in many lower executive (clerical supervisory) staff. SOPOM covers higher executive and managerial grades. Between the three groups there is little overlap in membership but intense rivalry and even bitterness is displayed in the attitudes of one towards the other.

On September 30, 1969, the Post Office Whitley system ceased to exist. It was replaced by a strange amalgam of procedures.

COPOU has recreated a staff side (now called "consortium") machinery with a national secretariat and subcommittee structure related to the main substantive issues and the representative strengths of the organisation. Beneath this is a two-tier structure of regional and local councils which relate to management units previously serviced by Whitley Councils. For its part the Post Office agreed to communicate with the nominated conveners of these councils on all matters of common concern to more than one COPOU affiliate. On matters affecting the members of only one union that body is consulted directly. In this way negotiations on such matters of pay increases based on local productivity all unions are treated in the same individual fashion and CPSA and SOPOM are on a level footing with the affiliates of COPOU. On other matters where discussion concerning grades covered by these latter unions also covers ground common to COPOU members the previously existing joint consultation and negotiating arrangements have been destroyed by the refusal of COPOU to enter joint discussions with the other unions. As a consequence the Post Office has now to negotiate or consult in triplicate on a wide range of issues.

The creation of a separate negotiating and consultative structure for higher management was largely engineered by the Post Office itself. The continued existence of the post and telecommunications section of CPSA is almost certainly not within the long-term plans of Post Office management. It is hardly fourteen years since a separate organisation for post and telegraphic clerks went out of existence, and the continued separate identity of clerical officers in CPSA is a constant source of irritation and perhaps emulation for white-collar workers in the UPW. Throughout the interunion negotiations leading up to the corporation Vesting Day management have reiterated their statement of neutrality. It is clear that they are now anxious to keep in check the latest CPSA claims for pay increases based on productivity for fear of handling any kind of temporary advantage to its clerical members.

On the other hand, white-collar workers in the Post Office appear to have acquired a new militancy in their pursuit of a separate identity and a separate means of representation. The outcome of these counteracting forces will very much depend on the way in which they are handled by union leaders. The CPSA is obviously reluctant to give up some 25,000 of its 180,000 membership and, in addition, to give up the opportunity of following its promoted members into supervisory ranks in which it is now recruiting for the first time. Yet UPW is itself facing considerable reductions in membership. As a result of mechanisation and automation the sorting grades, telegraphists, telephonists and counter clerks will be considerably reduced over the next decade. To leave other new and expanding fields of employment to another union—especially to the CPSA —would seem a somewhat altruistic decision for its leaders to take.

It is possible that, faced with a fragmented staff side, an increasingly price-conscious Post Office management may force bargaining close to plant or area management level. Once agreements become normal at this level it might be possible for them to develop procedures for the limited recognition of unions similar to those which exist at departmental level in the civil service. Thus it would be possible in some areas to recognise COPOU for all staff including a scattering of clerks. Such local recognition within particular bargaining units, in the American manner, might well find its way onto the statute book within the period of the present Conservative administration. If this happens it might encourage the Post Office management to modify the present centralised structure of bargaining. At this time, such possible strategies are, of course, mere speculation.

·V·

Industrial Relations in the Health Service

THE BACKGROUND TO THE NATIONAL HEALTH SERVICE AND SOME PRESENT PROBLEMS

THE National Health Service came into being on July 5, 1948, in accordance with the provisions of the National Health Service Act, 1946. Its amorphous shape reflected both the comprehensiveness of the ideals set out in the Beveridge Report "Full Employment in a Free Society" 1944 and the constraints set by the continued vested interests of existing public health bodies and occupational associations. Its function is to provide remedial and preventative medicine in all of its various forms and to complement the range of other social services being provided by central government, local authorities, and to a much less extent by charities.

It was brought into being by a Labour administration with a proclaimed belief in the need to "divorce the case of health from questions of personal means or other factors irrelevant to it and thus to encourage the obtaining of early advice and promotion of good health rather than only the treatment of ill health."[1]

This statement remains the measure against which the National Health Service is judged but it was in fact subjected to early modifications. The next Labour administration in 1950 was forced by rising costs and Korean War rearmament costs to introduce nominal charges for dental and opthalmic treatment and to give future governments the power to raise a small levy on the local dispensing of prescriptions. These monies, together with returns from the limited private services provided within hospitals (i.e. to a small proportion of patients who pay additional rates for nonprescribed private wards, etc.), account for under 4 percent of the finances. The small weekly

1. Quoted in "National Health Service Notes," Department of Health and Social Security, Information Division, 1970.

statutory subscription made by all working adults to the Central National Health Service Fund makes up about 10 percent of its annual income. This proportion has steadily declined throughout the life of the service and at the present time the major source of finance is the Treasury consolidated fund, i.e. general government income from all forms of taxation. In addition to the centrally provided finances local authority taxation ("rates" or property taxes) provided another sixth to the £1,274 millions spent by central government in the year 1967/68 making a total of £1,490 millions.

Though this sum represented the fourth largest item of public expenditure in that year, the relative cost of the service when expressed as a proposition of gross domestic product has remained remarkably constant at between 3.4 percent (1948) and 4 percent (1968). Both figures are less than for similar services provided in other advanced industrial countries, but in recent years proposals to increase the number of services for which fees are charged has been widely canvassed. The reasons for this are probably to be indicated by two statistics. In 1960/61 investment in new hospital equipment and building made up 3.5 percent of health expenditure; expenditure on general medical services nearly 12 percent. In 1968/69 the respective proportions are expected to be almost equal—nearly 8 percent has been spent on capital expenditure and less than 9 percent on medical services. Other specialist services have suffered a similar decline. While the massive investment program begun in 1964 has been partly financed out of a real increase in overall expenditure there has evidently been a considerable redistribution of resources away from current expenditure, an item in which fees, wages, and salaries make up the major proportion.

Another major critique directed at the service springs directly from the circumstances in which it was created. The criticisms have been expressed in several recent documents. One was the Salmon Report published in 1966. The main emphasis of the report was on the need to improve the quality of local management and to provide better management training for nurses.

Another was the, now abortive, parliamentary green paper

("National Health Service," February 1970) in which the last Labour administration expressed some preliminary proposals for reorganising the regional administrative structure of the service.

These proposals were essentially concerned with the improved integration of professional services beneath specialist management. This aim was present in the mind of the minister Aneurin Bevàn, in 1946 but was considerably modified in the years before 1948 to accommodate a whole range of existing institutions. Principal among these administrative interests were municipal (city) hospitals, a system dating from Queen Elizabeth I, and other local authority services such as maternity, child welfare, and public health nursing established during the last hundred years. More important however was the general practitioner service which was previously financed in two ways.

Under the provisions of the National Health Insurance Act 1911 all employees earning less than £420 (limit in 1948) had to make a weekly contribution to an approved fund which had to be matched by an employer contribution. Subscriptions to this fund were collected by any one of several "approved" societies (of which trade unions made up a large proportion). About one half the population received free medicine and the services of a physician as well as sick and unemployment pensions under this fairly comprehensive scheme. Other contingencies were covered by supplementary schemes similar to the Blue Cross. Thus many of the services provided within the present state scheme were previously bought by the patients in a direct or, in the latter case, an indirect manner.

Most general practitioners (family physicians) received a small proportion of their income in direct fees or consultancy fees, but they also received a steady income from a National health insurance (NHI) annual "retainer" paid on each NHI patient held on their books. This fee was paid from the National Health Insurance Fund irrespective of how many visits were made by or to the patient. The "capitation scheme" as it was called was carried into the National Health Service in 1948 as the basis for a compromise between bureaucratic control and professional autonomy upon which the new scheme became a political reality. General practitioners and consultants thus retained an "independent" market position as subcontractors which allowed them greater freedom as a body than would have been the case in salaried employment. Hence the blue prints for a locally integrated hospital and general practitioner service were shelved. Over the intervening period general practitioners have become isolated from changes in capital intensive diagnostic and remedial treatment which are just now being translated into public investment in new hospital plants. Not only has their remuneration tended to decline in real terms but so, paradoxically, has their role and status within the community.

THE ADMINISTRATIVE STRUCTURE

The National Health Service (NHS) is carried on through three separate channels which relate to the division of interests before its commencement. The first is that of the doctors and independent practitioners described above; these are covered by a largely autonomous channel of authority within the general medical services. Second, there is the organisation of the hospital and specialist service covering all forms of hospitals providing treatment for in-patients and out-patients. Last, there is a whole range of support services provided by local authorities. The previous emphasis in local authorities was clearly on the preventative, public health aspects of medicine. However the major function of local authorities today is to provide supportive services in terms of after-care treatment of clinical cases or the maintenance of the permanently disabled, aged, and with the mentally subnormal outside hospitals. Over the last decade there has been a movement towards the long-sought-after integrated system represented by 93 local health centres. Most local authority services are administered by the local medical officer of health (i.e. a qualified physician).

General practitioner services are controlled by local executive committees appointed by the minister who is advised by the professional associations appropriate to the appointment. With some exceptions, there is a separate council for each administrative county and county borough. Each council has thirty members who serve in a voluntary capacity: fifteen are nominated by local doctors, dentists, opticians, and pharmacists, eight by the local health authority and seven by the minister. In organising the provision of general medical services, the council consults a local body recognised by the minister as representative of doctors.

A practitioner is employed by contract with the executive council to provide certain services within the area in which he has set up his practice. The form of contract is uniform within occupations, though varying in a nationally agreed manner between regions. For all such occupations it contains a "per capita" element of payment but the total number of separate practices (i.e. separate establishments) working within the NHS is strictly controlled by the local executive council. Competition is kept to a minimum but where possible councils attempt to retain consumer choice. New applications to provide a medical service are vetted by the local professional body and are then forwarded by the local executive committee to a national vetting body, the medical practices committee. This committee is also appointed by the minister and consists of a doctor as chairman, six other doctors, and two laymen. The committee keeps a constant survey of the need for doctors and classifies areas accordingly. The administration of the hospital and specialists services in England and Wales is largely in the hands of fifteen regional hospital boards (RHBs) appointed directly by the minister (the Secretary of State for Health). These boards are responsible to the ministry for the preparation of long term policy in respect to the provision of hospital services in their respective geographical areas. They also have powers over the appointment of consultant staff and some control over the outside servicing of hospitals by other parts of the NHS. These boards have in turn appointed 332 hospital management committees (HMCs) to be responsible for individual or groups of hospitals. There are in all 2,368 hospitals run by HMCs. Appointments to RHBs are made from panels made up of names put forward by political parties, trade unions employers, associations, and other important groups representative in the appropriate region. Appointments to HMCs include nominees from elected members of local authorities (though they are not appointed in that capacity). In addition 36 institutional groups have been designated as teaching hospitals and are in the charge of autonomous boards of governors. Their status is very much like that of universities and indeed their teaching staffs are now covered by the national negotiating machinery for university teachers rather than by NHS machinery. The governors of the teaching hospitals are appointed by the minister and their role combines the powers of regional boards and hospital management committees. In this instance the advice of professional bodies, particularly the Royal Colleges of Physicians and of Surgeons and the Royal College of Nursing are important in making appointments since these hospitals provide important points of entry into their respective occupations. These groups contain 143 separate hospitals.

Within the hospitals themselves there are further divisions of authority. There is generally no single executive manager. In a typical HMC group of hospitals, management is divided between the chief lay officer (the group secretary), the chief nursing officer and a coalition of senior medical staff who may or may not have institutionalised means of coordination.

The third branch of the Health Service is unified under the major local authorities which were designated as "local health authorities" under the 1946 Act. Each of these has a statutory duty to provide inter alia, maternity, child welfare and home nursing services, health visiting, and vaccination. In addition to these and other statutory functions health authorities are empowered to organise home help and care and after-care services. In the provision of these services increasing emphasis is being placed on the facilities of voluntary organisations.

THE EMPLOYMENT STRUCTURE

The employment structure of the National Health Service may be divided into three main groups: the hospital and specialist services which operate from hospital premises, the general medical services which include general practitioners (family physicians), dentists, pharmacists, ophthalmic medical practitioners and opticians, and other professional services employed on a subcontractual fee-paying or per capita basis; and local health authorities. The breakdown in total employment of all main occupational groups on December 31, 1968, is shown in Table 4.

Table 4.
Employment in the National Health Service

Hospital and specialist services	Whole-time	Part-time
Medical and dental	21,232	5,841
Nursing and midwifery	188,888	79,235
Nursing cadets	7,430	235
Other professional and technical	31,693[1]	—
Blood transfusion centres	2,215	331
Mass radiography staff	554	63
Administrative and clerical	35,307	7,030
Maintenance, storekeeper transport and domestic workers (ancillary staffs)	152,573	66,548
Family practitioner services		
General practitioners	21,410[1]	
General dental practitioners	110,593[1]	
Ophthalmic medical practitioners and opticians	7,057[1]	
Local health authority services		
Domiciliary midwifes	3,406	3,608
Home nurses	6,470	4,492
Health visitors, etc.	1,199	6,802
Chiropodists	442	2,959
Nursery nurses	5,802	
Mental health therapy and training	1,215	3,012
Ambulance personnel	15,000[1]	
Home helps	2,966	65,129
Ancillary staff	30,000[2]	20,000
	545,452	265,285

1. Hours worked by part-time workers are consolidated into whole-time equivalents and cannot be separated out of available data.
2. Author's estimate of division between whole-time and part-time.
Source: Data are based on the Annual Report of the Department of Health and Social Security 1968 HMSO Cmnd. 4100.

The Status of the Health Employee

With the exception of the ministerial staff employed at departmental level, NHS employees are not usually regarded as civil servants. (For certain technical purposes they have been temporarily so regarded at certain times and purposes, for example under the provisions of the 1966 Prices and Incomes Act.) In general, health employees are subject to no more statutory limitations upon their rights as citizens than any other public employees. That is to say that under the 1896 Conciliation Act it might be said that withdrawal of their labour was "endangering human life or property." However no action has been taken by the government in numerous recent strike actions in the public utilities and it seems unlikely that this is a real constraint upon the actions of a health employee. His civic rights may be diminished if he is a local authority employee, since he will be unable to retain his employment if elected to the local (city) council. Yet under the generally applicable rules contained in National Health Service conditions of service all employees are entitled to special leave of absence in order to serve as local councillors (subject to local conditions) and special leave to stand as candidates in national Parliamentary elections.

Salaried or wage earning Health employees have an individual contract with either a regional hospital board, a teaching hospital, or with a local authority as the case may be. General practitioners are self-employed, but the terms under which their services are employed by the NHS are such that in order to take any appointment it (the appointment) must be first approved by the local executive council and of course the practitioner's qualifications must be such as to meet the requirements of the same body. Consultants are normally employed under contract to the regional hospital board or teaching hospital.

In practice, entrance to posts accounting for about half the total work force as set out in Table 4 is affected by membership of a professional association. Some twenty-two associations are recognised by the department for the purposes of registering formally qualified recruits for their particular occupation. Most important of the professional institutions which work in liaison with the NHS are the General Medical Council and the General Nursing Council. These councils have statutory responsibility for the organisation of the training of doctors and nurses respectively (separate machinery existing for Scotland and Northern Ireland).

The councils determine age of entry and required entry qualifications, draw up training, syllabuses, and set the standard for qualification. They finance much of the training available to would-be registered doctors and nurses with the aid of State funds. They are also responsible for the maintenance of professional conduct within and outside of the service: to be struck off the professional register or roll is to lose one's right to practice in that occupation. Hence the statutory limitations upon the rights and responsibilities of many health service employees is secondary to the superior discipline of their closed society.

THE ESTABLISHMENT OF NEGOTIATING MACHINERY

Prior to 1948 some sections of health employment were already covered by joint committees and councils established for the purposes of collective bargaining or consultation between employing bodies and trade unions or professional associations. Between 1946 and 1948 the transition to a unified negotiating structure was consistent upon the redefinition of these employing units and the identification of the status of hitherto autonomous professional interests within the new structure. The model taken for the establishment of bargaining machinery was that of the Whitley Council already operating with great success in the civil service. The diversity of interests which had to be accommodated in the Health Service was such, however, as to impose a much greater complexity upon the eventually agreed structure.

By the late 1930s many of the local authority and voluntary hospitals were heavily dependent upon centrally provided finance, and for this reason the government's influence in setting up central consultative machinery during World War II was very important. The first of these bodies had been set up after World War I but had only limited powers to recommend new rates of pay or changes in working conditions to employing bodies. In 1920 a Joint Conciliation Committee was also formed for mental hospital nurses and domestic workers by their large authority employers acting under the aegis of the ministry. Founded in 1910, an Asylum-Workers Union grew rapidly and in 1919 began a series of recognition strikes and actions in support of national awards of the conciliation committee. By World War II the recommendations of this body were generally observed. A second board was formed to consider and recommend raises in the pay of the administrative and clerical staff in mental hospitals who were also represented by their own national association.

Meanwhile, attempts at national Whitleyism in the rest of local government employment were being pursued. No real headway was made in union attempts to extend this machinery to the hospitals. Mental nursing was largely a male profession often employing people with wider industrial experience and an ability to organise the efforts of less educated domestic workers. If conditions in most hospitals were rigorous, in mental hospitals they were usually regimental and often hazardous. Women and girls in the nursing occupations were, and are, much more difficult to organise in unions.

In 1941 the Ministry of Health took a unilateral decision to guarantee minimum salaries for student nurses whose exploitation had become notorious. The minister did this by agreeing to pay for half the raise from Treasury funds. In the same year the government appointed the Nurses Salaries Committee (Rushcliffe) "to draw up, as soon as possible, agreed scales and emoluments for State Registered Nurses employed in England and Wales in hospitals and in public services, including district nurses and for Student Nurses in hospitals approved as training schools by the General Nursing Council for England and Wales." A similar committee was appointed for Scotland. The Committee was made up of employers' representatives from the British Hospitals Association (teaching and independent), local authorities, and a large professional employer. The Royal College of Nursing took on an official negotiating role for the first time sitting with the National Association of Local Government Officers and TUC representatives on staff side of the committee. It did so only reluctantly after resisting any form of negotiating structure for some years previously. The clinching factor was the continued government offer to subsidize pay raises. In its actions towards the nurses, as to all health staff, the ministry was acting under emergency wartime powers by which it was expected to provide an immediate and comprehensive service to civilians under enemy attack.

THE STRUCTURE AND SCOPE OF WHITLEYISM

Coincidental with the introduction of the National Health Service came a system of Whitley Councils designed to (1) "secure the greatest possible measure of cooperation between the authorities responsible for the nation's health and the general body of persons engaged in the health services, with a view to increased efficiency in the public service, and the well-being of those engaged in the services"; and (2) "to provide machinery for the consideration of remuneration and conditions of service" of health service employees, clerical and administrative employees of local health authorities, together with domestic and (up to 1970) ancillary staff employed in residential institutions run by local authorities.[2] Formally, then, the functions of Whitleyism in the NHS are similar to those in the civil service, i.e. to provide a means of collective bargaining in which consultation or "cooperative bargaining" is seen to be the main activity undertaken by the actors. There are two important differences. One is the existence of a separate grievance procedure in the NHS; the other is the lack of any specific arbitration procedure outside that provided in the Conciliation Act 1896 and Industrial Courts Act 1919 for all forms of employment. The organisation of the service in Scotland differs in some respects from that in England and Wales, but the differences are of no significance in relation to the Whitley structure so that references are only made to the latter in the English context.

In 1946 the Ministry of Health initiated procedural discussions with the professional associations and trade unions by placing before them a suggested structure which, with some modifications, was eventually accepted by most of the principal actors who now participate in the machinery. It consists of a General

2. Main Constitution of the Whitley Councils for the Health Service (Great Britain): Appendix to "Conditions of Service" March 1, 1968, Ministry of Health, R.S. 1(C).

Council and nine functional councils relating to the main occupational groups shown in Table 4. The councils are shown in Table 5.

Table 5.
NHS Whitley Councils

	Staff Covered
Administrative and Clerical	58,000
Ancillary Staffs	216,000
Dental (Local Authorities)	1,600
Medical and (Hospital) Dental	25,220
Nurses and Midwives	274,000
Optical	110
Pharmaceutical	1,700
Professional and Technical A	15,800
Professional and Technical B	18,000

Each functional council is responsible for determining the remuneration within the occupations defined by the General Council as being within its purview and the conditions of service peculiar to persons in those occupations (within professional limitations). The General Council has two major purposes. One, already alluded to, is that of policing the structure and providing modifications to the machinery where it feels changes to be required. Procedural changes negotiated within the General Council include the establishment of the grievance procedure and the addition of local consultative machinery.

The second and quantitatively more important activity of the General Council is negotiating on all matters concerning allowances and special rates of pay over and above those negotiated in functional councils together with leave, redundancy arrangements, and other conditions uniform to salaried or wage earning staff. Exceptions to the scope of negotiations include superannuation arrangements which as in the civil service are determined by act of Parliament and are therefore the subject of considerable pressure group activity by unions and professional associations. At all levels it is difficult to distinguish when interchange is taking the form of negotiation and when it is consultation. Lack of any definition of an arbitrable item makes this distinction even more difficult in the NHS than in the civil service.

Negotiations and consultations take place with individual unions and association outside of the Whitley councils as in other areas of public employment. Such matters may be procedural, for example the negotiation of a check-off system, or substantive, as for example in the case of the training and grading structure of particular occupations.

THE CONSTITUTION AND AUTHORITY OF THE WHITLEY COUNCILS AND COMMITTEES

The General Council consists of 55 members of whom 27 represent the employing authorities and 28 the employees and those with constructural arrangements. On the employers' side the ministry retains 5 seats, regional hospital boards 5, teaching hospitals 2, hospital management committees 3, executive councils 3, local authorities 9. The staff side is elected not by individual constituent bodies but as representatives of the functional councils. Of these the Ancillary Staffs Council has 5 seats, the Administrative and Clerical Council, the Medical and (Hospital) Dental Council, and the Nurses and Midwives Council have 4 each, the two Professional and Technical Councils and the Pharmaceutical Council have 3 each, and Local Authority Dentists and the Optical Council have one each. Functional councils are left to make their own arrangements in respect to these nominations which are made annually. In the case of the medical and dental councils the issue of representation is in little doubt since the staff side of these functional councils is wholly dominated by a single professional body. But in most other councils uneasy alliances between professional associations serve to lessen union influence at national level. Only on the ancillary staffs councils are unions in control of staff side.

The numbers of seats on functional councils approximate the size of the occupational groups represented with some adjustments made to meet the need to incorporate certain unions and, more particularly, the more numerous small professional associations. The smallest council is the Dental Council comprising 27 seats—9 on the management side made up of the County Councils Association, the Association of Municipal Corporations, the Greater London Council and two Scottish local authority associations. All of the 12 seats on staff side are occupied by the British Dental Association. The largest council is the Nurses and Midwives Council comprising 64 seats, 23 on the management side and 41 on the staff side. The management side comprises a similar range of local authority representatives together with the regional and hospital management boards, and the Department of Health. On staff side, the Royal College of Nursing predominates with 12 representatives, the Royal College of Midwives has 6 seats, and the remainder are distributed between 4 unions and 6 quasi-professional protective associations representing matrons, senior midwives, health visitors, public health officers, and welfare administrators. The composition of these councils represents extremes in variety and numbers of participants as well as the extremes of size.

The formal procedure for all Whitley Councils is extremely liberal. Chairmen are chosen alternatively from management and staff side. Secretaries are appointed by both sides and may or may not be council members. Representatives may be co-opted in a consultative (nonvoting) capacity for discussions on subjects in which the represented organisations have an interest. Meetings may be held as often as required but decisions must, as in the civil service, be arrived at by consensus and with concurrence of both sides. At times when key negotiations are taking place meetings are often adjourned and may continue over a period of days. More usually business is carried out in subcommittees.

The most important of the subcommittees are those formed for the negotiation of special conditions relating to particular forms of employment. The Building Craftsman's Committee of the Ancillary Staffs Council is one example but the three committees for the determination of working conditions for physicians are potentially of crucial importance. These are Committee A for general practitioners, Committee B for medical practitioners employed by or in contract with regional hospital boards or HMCs, and Committee C for physicians employed by or in contract with local authorities. In practice Committee A has never functioned for reasons explained below; the latter committees function very much along the lines and with the status of separate councils. So also do the subcommittees of the Pharmaceutical Council which deal with the contractual terms of independent retail chemists (drug stores) on one hand and with the salaries and conditions of service of full-time pharmacists in hospitals and health centres on the other.

The ultimate authority for the imposition of agreements made within the Whitley machinery rests with the minister (the Secretary of State for Health and Security) who is empowered by section 66 of the National Health Act 1946 to make regulations in respect of the qualifications, remuneration, and conditions of all employees within the NHS. Hence decisions arrived at in Whitley Council must be approved by the minister before passing into effect. For some years an internal controversy focussed around the issue of whether the decisions of functional councils could be passed to the minister before being approved by the General Council. This matter resolved itself in the late 1950s when a number of functional council awards were being delayed in the General Council by tactical manoeuvres by one or other section of management side (particularly the ministry) or by professional associations. Since that time the constitution has been interpreted in such a way as to allow the minister to accept the recommendations of functional councils.

In 1951 it was found that some hospitals were "bidding up" the Whitley awards using national rates as the basis for local negotiations or offers to new recruits. For this reason the National Health Service (Remuneration and Conditions of Service) Regulations were passed in Parliament. These stipulated that the pay of any officer belonging to a class whose rates of remuneration has been determined through the approved channels of negotiation and authorised by the minister should be "neither more nor less than the remuneration so approved." The provision ensured that control over rates of earnings rested with the management side of Whitley—and, quite incidentally, with those unions and associations which had achieved recognition both within the Whitley procedures and in the ad hoc machinery with which it was supplemented.

THE COMPOSITION AND AUTHORITY OF THE MANAGEMENT SIDE

Throughout the early years of the NHS the management side was heavily weighted towards the ministry (8 seats on each council) and local authorities, who had all the seats on the Dental Council, and 44 overall other councils as against only 54 for the regional boards and boards of governors combined, the latter even being very poorly represented on the important Ancillary Staffs and Nurses and Midwives Councils. In 1948 the boards employed four fifths of the total health service staffs as against the one fifth in local authorities. As a result staff side were not negotiating with representative management members. It seemed clear that central and local government representatives were themselves full-time government officials whose appointment expressed the preoccupation of the minister with the retention of control over public expenditure. The result of this and the delaying tactics of some members of the General Council was to induce the House of Commons Select Committee on Estimates to condemn the "inordinate delays in reaching decisions" in a report during 1952.

In 1956 an investigatory committee (Guilleband) appointed by a Conservative administration to review the increasing cost of the health service advised that ministerial representation should be reduced. This advice was accepted and subsequently there has been a redistribution of seats in favour of the boards. The situation is by no means settled. Proposals put forward under the last Labour government for the reform of local government and the abolition of regional boards as they exist at the moment contained an opportunity to rid the Whitley management side of vested interests represented in the present multitiered structure of local authorities.

The staff side continue to complain that without Treasury representation they are negotiating with a management side which lacks authority. In particular the record of staff successes in the arbitration decisions of the Industrial Court is quoted as representing the strength of Treasury influence in departmental decisions.

Unlike the Whitley structure in the civil service and Post Office there is no permanent machinery in the Health Service within which to negotiate over the implementation of application of National Whitley awards. Since the environmental conditions in which the agreement has to be implemented are extremely diverse this variety of itself provides a reason for delay in the negotiation of agreements. When agreements come to be put into practice it is extremely difficult to control the manner of their implementation as handled in the complex division of authority in hospital service. Without an efficient servicing and policing of agreements by the unions or by the professional associations, the improvements in working conditions and even pay can be and often are diluted at local levels. This may even occur with the approval of the ministry as happened recently when the board and lodging costs charged to trainee and other residential nurses in hospital were raised to an amount about equal to a pay raise.

The minister is not only represented on all the Whitley Councils with the exception of the Dental Council, he is also the final arbiter on all agreements reached in the councils and other negotiating bodies within the service and his powers of veto extend to arbitration awards. This clearly reflects on the role of arbitration. Up to 1957 from time to time ministers had assured staff side that their powers were mere formalities and that their use would be "a complete contradiction" of Whitleyism. However the first tentative attempts at incomes policy introduced by the Conservative administration in 1956 were applied with particular severity to the public services. This resulted in the first attempt to intervene in the award of a review body on doctors' and dentists' remuneration and a complete veto on agreements made within the Administrative and Clerical council. In the first case action by the general practitioners resulted in a modified award; clerical employees were forced to repeat their claim and after prolonged haggling over the terms of reference this claim was presented to an Industrial Court some eight months later. The subsequent award, a compromise weighted towards the staff claim, was accepted by the minister. Subsequently the minister has delayed or reduced a number of awards, the latest being that of the standing review body on doctors and dentists' remuneration which was first delayed and then reduced in June and July 1970. All of these actions have taken place within the increasing formality of a national incomes policy.

THE ATTITUDE OF MANAGEMENT

The Ancillary Staffs Council was the first council to operate; the transfer of functions from a former Joint Negotiating Committee set up in 1945 was a relatively smooth process as was the case with clerical and administrative staff. In other cases the decision as to what organisations should represent which employees did not immediately bring inter-staff side squabbles to an end. The two-sided conflict remains present on both sides of the Whitley Council, on staff side between professional association and trade union and on management side between lay representatives and professionals lining up against "men from the ministry." The result is not one management attitude but at least two, that of the local administration and that of the ministry.

There has certainly been no general encouragement to join unions and, at first, only a somewhat ambivalent attitude towards the concept of Whitleyism. This ambivalence sprang from two sources. There was as little desire on the part of the local lay management committees to recognise unions and to be governed by a nationally agreed rate of remuneration as there had been among local authority employees. The attempts to set up national Whitleyism in this latter area of employment broke down in 1921 (one year after its initiation) and it was not finally established until after the unions forced employers into compulsory arbitration in 1941 under the wartime provisions of the Employment and National Arbitration Order 1305. Often the local dignitaries who had been involved in this event were the same people who spoke for hospital boards and local authorities in the new Health Service.

Second, the finally agreed administrative structure of the service was such as to give doctors and senior nurses considerable decision-making capacity. Neither group was sympathetic to unions, identifying them as both a threat to their professional status and as outposts of the administration which had imposed the NHS upon them. As a result unions met with lack of cooperation on the part of management at both the local and the national level. A much greater rapport existed between professional associations and management side on some councils, a feeling engendered by the degree to which professionals cooperated with lay representatives within local management. In this sense professionals and the "public" representatives sometimes form a common front against the ministry on the General Council, a division which runs across the formal lines of demarcation between staff and management.

There is a generally held view among trade union representatives that staff-management relationships have improved and that the professional-union conflict within the councils has reduced over the last twenty-two years. This is taking the long view: at present Whitleyism in the NHS does not express the same degree of commitment to management consultation and the concept of employee participation that exists in the civil service.

RECOGNITION AND THE COMPOSITION OF STAFF SIDE

The 1946 National Health Act contained no statutory imposition of the employers' duty to bargain nor guidance on recognition procedures. In part this may have been due to lack of government experience in formal labour relations outside of the relatively unstructured civil service Whitley machinery. It is more likely that the need to persuade professional interests to organise themselves in a manner suitable for inclusion in the Whitley staff side led the minister to conclude that informality was the more viable approach to the problem of recognition. A number of the major associations including the British Medical Association (BMA) and the Royal College of Nursing actively campaigned against the proposed structure of labour relations and indeed the former body continues its refusal to represent general practitioners on Whitley Councils despite the existence of a committee structure. In these circumstances the drafting of criteria for recognition might well have become a separate area of disagreement on the wide front along which the minister was conducting negotiations with the professional associations.

Since that time no major modifications have taken place in the structure and composition of staff representation. Although there is no formal acknowledgement of the right of Whitley staff sides to control entry to the machinery it is clear that the existing bodies exercise considerable influence over the minister in taking decisions on fresh applications for recognition, if only because they have been refused. A number of organisations in the medical and nursing profession were refused recognition or received only limited recognition prior to 1948. The British Medical Association was, for example, well established as the spokesman of the medical profession before the introduction of the NHS. Its real strength lay among general practitioners of whom some 84 percent were in the membership of the association. It came to prominence in the organisation of resistance to the 1911 National Insurance Act which brought general practitioners under contract to the State and subsequently led two mass resignations in support of claims for increased fees. Yet it also has many consultants and specialists in membership.

Its pre-eminence was recognised in the majority of seats it obtained on Whitley Medical Council but the rest went to a consortium made up of the Royal Colleges, Scottish Corporations (bodies of similar professional status), and the consultants and specialists, all of whom felt a need to be separately represented. However, within the special committees formed by the BMA as their links with the Whitley Council machinery (for reasons explained below) there were incorporated additional representatives of the Medical Practitioners Union, a small registered trade union for doctors affiliated to the TUC. This body has recently (1970) affiliated with the Association of Scientific Technical and Managerial Staffs (ASTMS), a general white-collar union, which has thus obtained minority rights in the representation of doctors. In 1963 a small breakaway organisation from the BMA, the General Practitioners Association, was formed after a disappointing award. This association continues despite its failure to obtain ministerial recognition.

The most recent major breakaway attempt was made among ambulance men who are not covered by the bargaining procedures of the Health Service but by the National Joint Industrial Council for Local Authority Services (Manual Workers). A local strike of ambulance men in London during August 1969 turned into a national action in support of the Federation's claim for recognition on the NJIC. It was eventually agreed by the employers and already recognised unions (excluding the Federation) to refer the dispute to an independent one-man inquiry. The mediator chosen, Dr. W. J. M. McCarthy, suggested that the Federation's claim for recognition should be refused but that a new system of negotiation and consultation should be evolved for ambulance personnel in which the Federation might gain a place as a professionally representative body in the organisation of training, etc. The Federation's allegation that each of the major three unions organising ambulance men had no more than two or three thousand of such personnel in membership was rejected by McCarthy, but little published evidence of their true membership exists. The criteria which emerged from the report of the enquiry discount the special interests of the breakaway union members against the superior resources and bargaining expertise available to them in the established unions. "The fact is that the ambulance service may be a social world of its own; but it is not an economic or managerial island."[3]

The negotiations before 1948 resulted in the recognition of eleven registered unions and forty professional bodies. Most of the latter adopted a "protective" or collective bargaining role only at the introduction of the Whitley machinery. The con-

3. W. E. J. McCarthy, "Representation and Collective Bargaining in the Ambulance Service." A report undertaken for and published by the National Joint Council for Local Authorities Services (Manual Workers).

stitution of staff side of the several councils also contains the representatives of self-employed contractors. The form of this representation on behalf of medical practitioners has already been described but on other councils, such as the Pharmaceutical Council, extends to that of large employers of pharmacists such as the Company Chemists Association Ltd. and the Co-operative Union Ltd.

The recognition of these bodies has extended from 1948 to the present day with little alteration and no extension to others. All of the six major unions on the Whitley staff side are affiliated to the TUC. Only one, the Confederation of Health Service Employees (approximately 40,000 members), confines its recruitment to the Health Service: it holds seats on the Ancillary Staffs Council which sets the pay and conditions for most manual workers in the service. Its members are also to be found among nurses and midwives, the administrative and clerical staff, professional and technical staff, and hospital pharmaceutical assistants. The National Union of Public Employees represents all but the latter group on the appropriate councils having some 112,000 members in the Health Service and some 200,000 in local authorities. The bulk of its members are among manual employees; most white-collar unionists are in the National and Local Government Officers' Association (NALGO) with some 35,000 NHS members which it represents on the Nurses and Midwives Council, the Professional and Technical Council A (i.e. for technicians and supportive professional grades such as almoners and occupational therapists), and on the Clerical and Administrative Council where it predominates with 12 out of the available 30 seats. The other white-collar union, the Association of Scientific, Technical, and Managerial Staffs, organises the groups distinguished in its title across all sectors of employment. It obtained a small footing in hospital laboratories between the wars and is now present in both Professional and Technical Councils A and B (the latter covering hospital scientists and technicians having no direct patient contact) and on the Pharmaceutical and Optical Councils. A large counter clerks union, USDAW, also sits on the last three councils, and two large general unions—the GMWU and TGWU—are represented elsewhere. The GMWU has significant numbers of members among clerks and nurses as well as among manual and domestic staff; their health membership amounts to about 20,000 as against the TGWU's 15,000.

The overlap in the fields of union recruitment is considerable, and there was a great deal of competition for members during the early days of the Health Service. At length interunion agreements were drawn up on the basis of which the manual unions affiliated to the TUC agreed to spheres of influence defined in terms of hospitals in which their membership already existed. Competition continues in many hospitals, particularly among the newly union conscious nursing occupations. Yet there are many establishments and even more occupational groups in which union penetration is minimal. Union representation at local level is patchy and the antiunion attitudes of local hospital management and the staff themselves are a fundamental block to recruitment. Overall membership of registered trade unions in the NHS amounts to not much more than 18 percent, but among manual workers the proportion could be as high as 75 percent.

Perhaps the greatest source of weakness originating from the jurisdictional overlap among unions is to be found *outside* the Whitley Councils. As in other federal arrangements in the public services, representative organisations can negotiate separately and can be recognised for representative functions outside the Whitley machinery. Only three union groups can claim to speak authoritatively in separate discussions.

One such group is the Confederation of Health Service Employees, which has inherited the representative role created by the Mental Hospitals Association in the 1920 Joint Conciliation Council for Mental Hospitals. The National Federation of Building Operatives, largely a craft organisation, represents most maintenance workers within a separate subcommittee of the Ancillary Staffs Council, while outside the Whitley machinery the engineering and electrical craft unions conduct separate negotiations with the employers to ensure the maintenance of the craft rates.

However, on only two councils, the Ancillary Staffs and

the Administrative and Clerical Councils, could unions gain an absolute majority by combining their joint representation. The multitude of professional interests that gained seats on Whitley Councils before 1948 hold a majority of seats on most other councils. These, more than multiunionism, make the formation of a unified staff side of the civil service kind an impossible goal to achieve in the Health Service. Professional associations which can claim a double loyalty among large numbers of health employees are obviously in a very strong position to carry on negotiations outside of the Whitley machinery. Together they control the quite separate system of councils established for the maintenance of professional standards. Such discussions give them an edge over the unions when they come to adopt their "protective" as against their "qualifying" or "learned society" role.

Some are debilitated by numbers within Whitley Councils in exactly the same manner as the unions. This is especially true in the Optical Council where retailing businesses, unions, professional associations, and the Worshipful Company of Spectacle Makers amount to thirteen separate representative organisations within staff side. In spite of the fact that professional associations make up the largest numbers on the functional councils they are usually representing single occupational groups, even when these amount to no more than small enclaves. Their obvious course of action is to negotiate on all important matters outside of Whitley.

There are two major problems faced by professional associations in undertaking a negotiating role. The first is a legal one which has been circumvented by those associations which now exist within the Whitley machinery. Under the 1871 Trade Union Act as amended by the acts of 1896 and 1913 trade unions whose statutory objects are defined as "the regulation of relations between workmen and masters" are exempt from most of the legal liabilities placed upon companies (corporations). In this way they have been excluded from civil actions for breach of contract. Most professional associations are, on the other hand, registered as companies. Furthermore a proviso is often included in their "memoranda of association" which prevents such associations from pursuing any trade union activity.

For some associations the way out was found very simply by creating a new body to which all their existing members were automatically affiliated. This is the case, for example, with the British Medical Association which created two bodies, the General Medical Services Committee and the Public Health Committee.

On the other hand the Institute of Medical Laboratory Technology refused a place on the Joint Negotiating Committee (Hospital Staffs) in 1945. In 1948 prior to the NHS it consented to the representation of its members on a separate negotiating body by a group of unions including the Association of Scientific Workers whose membership among these grades was relatively small. It retained its professional function of training and qualifying entrants to these technician grades.

The more important constraint on the bargaining activity of professional bodies is the reservations of their members towards anything that appears to give them a trade union image. This is especially true of senior members of professions who tend to be in administrative or employer roles. This tension between old and young members is not unusual within professional bodies but in the Health Service, registrars, senior house physicians, and matrons are acting as senior management within large plants. Their junior employees are sometimes as alienated from management as any industrial worker, yet their training and qualification is within the control of the senior members of their profession. Professional decisions are directly translated into the formal rules of very large employing organisations and gain much greater potency as a result. In particular most junior physicians and all junior nurses are still "trainees" in the sense that their hospital experience will be taken into account in any assessment leading to final qualification. For example, until recently the pay of nursing cadets was described as a "students' allowance."

Over the last decade the frustrations of junior hospital doctors have become such that they have formed a breakaway organisation from the BMA, the Junior Hospital Doctors' Association

(JHDA). At first this organisation's main concern was with the long periods of shift and weekend work done by hospital registrars and probationers, but their demands very quickly extended to include representation within discussions that the BMA and the Royal Colleges were having with the minister about career structures and post-graduate training. The BMA responded in the time-approved manner by reforming its internal structure to provide for an internal council for young doctors. Shortly after the establishment of this council in 1968 some of its members, many of whom had dual membership of the BMA and JHDA, adjourned the council *sine die*. Concurrently a letter to *The Times* (November 28, 1969) expressed their fears at the suggestion that the General Medical Council (the qualifying body of the profession and within the NHS) should be given statutory powers to make changes in the administration of qualifying boards. It suggested "that the standards of the profession must be defined by the democratically elected representatives of the profession alone." From subsequent indications of support received by the BMA it appears probable that the latter still commands the backing of most of the profession. Many of the present problems of young doctors are connected with market shortages and administrative inefficiencies in the hospital service. Both can be attributed at least in part to past actions of the BMA. The latter greatly influenced the first major attempt at manpower planning for physicians and as late as 1962 the BMA expressed fears of future unemployment among doctors.[4]

The role of the nurses associations in staff management relations is of course crucial. Not only are nurses by far the largest single occupational group, but the organisational and market pressures which operate upon junior doctors at a single stage in their career are much more applicable to nurses throughout their working life. Though a comparatively young profession —the Royal College of Nursing (RCN) received its charter

4. "Report of the Committee to Consider the Future Numbers of Medical Practitioners and the Appropriate Intake of Medical Students" (Sir Henry Willink Committee), HMSO, 1951. Also *The Times*, May 11, 1962, and Dr. R. G. Gibson, *British Medical Journal, Supplement ii*, July 26, 28, 1962.

in 1928—its very youth and "marginality" makes it extremely sensitive towards the status and prestige attributed to those holding nursing qualifications. These are awarded by the General Nursing Council, a body which, unlike the General Medical Council, is elected by and from the current body of registered nurses together with a minority of government-appointed lay representatives, and dates from 1920.

The Royal College was by no means the only representative of nurses in existence before 1948, and indeed it had been waging a constant war with at least two other professional associations. Nor was it representative of as many nurses as its allocation of seats on the Whitley Council indicated, but having opposed all attempts to establish negotiating machinery in the past it made common policy with the Royal College of Midwives and the other professional associations in gaining a preponderance of representation in the functional council. Its views on nurses' remuneration were expressed to a government committee of inquiry in 1938: "The payment of high salaries to student nurses is not recommended, as it is believed that this does not tend to attract the most suitable type of candidae."[5]

This was still the RCN's view in the negotiations prior to and in the early years of Whitleyism and still recurs in its arguments. The acceptance of the notion that young nurses are students rather than employees is of course central to the position of the RCN relative to trade unions.

Trade union activity among nurses has an intermittent history from about 1918. In 1937 the TUC took an initiative in bringing together existing affiliated unions who were attempting to organise nurses, behind a "TUC Charter for Nurses." Under trade union pressure the government agreed to set up the Athlone Committee of Inquiry into nurses' conditions (see footnote 5). The next initiative came in 1950 when the Confederation of Health Service Employees put itself at the head of protesting student nurses in demonstrations throughout the country. Na-

5. The Royal College of Nursing: Memorandum Relating to Conditions in the Nursing Profession for Submission to the Inter-Departmental Committee on the Nursing Services, January 1938, p. 6.

turally the RCN condemned their actions, but over the intervening years it has been forced to pay greater attention to the conditions of young nurses within the Whitley machinery. It still maintains its greatest influence on their career structure through elected representatives on the General Nursing Council. Generally its views have been expressed in regularly produced reports on training and job content rather than on pay and conditions. Its major strategy in this regard has been to restrict entrance to the profession, a policy which has been under increasing strain for some twenty-five years. In 1943 a second grade of "state enrolled" nurses was introduced to implement that of the "state registered" nurse, the new grade requiring lower educational qualifications and shorter training. In recent years an increasing amount of work is being done by unqualified nursing auxiliaries and nursing assistants. Qualified nursing has tended to become a supervisory occupation.

Over the last twenty years a form of whip-sawing has occurred in nurses' salaries as unions have supported increases for younger nurses and allowances for specialised nursing, such as mental nursing, while the ministry, through management side, has kept down concomitant increases for higher grade nurses. Most early claims were made for flat monetary increases rather than percentage increases in the rates of senior nurses. As a result differentials within the service were greatly eroded. The RCN has been concerned to restore these to pre-NHS levels and for short periods they have succeeded. Unfortunately for them the floor of salaries paid to trainee nurses has been so low that any change in the cost of living brings distress to these grades and results in pressures from below. These pressures express themselves in the usual manner, by increasingly frequent public demonstrations and by a rapidly climbing quit-rate. Over a third of the current intake of student nurses do not complete their training and intake figures have declined.

In 1961 staff side asked for a major reconstruction of the nurses' scales averaging a 35 percent increase overall. The claim coincided with the "pay pause" imposed by the government in that year. Five months later management offered a flat rate increase of 2.5 percent from the end of the pause in

April 1962. There followed one of the most successful of public campaigns to be organised by employee organisations in postwar Britain in which the Royal College and the unions did nothing to detract from the others' efforts or to lessen their impact on the public. Eventually an award of the Industrial Court in August 1962 gave an interim increase of 7.5 percent retrospective to April and ordered the two sides to negotiate.

By 1964 nurses' salaries were comparable with those in similar occupations outside the service, but the unevenness with which the government's incomes restraint was applied in 1966 took the relative earnings position of the nurses back to 1961. The Royal College launched a campaign for a £1 increase in the "training allowance" (the weekly wage) of student and pupil nurses. Eventually they were awarded one eighth of this amount, a sum contemptuously described as a "tea allowance." The staff side of the Nurses and Midwives Council were once more forced into cooperation in a public campaign for a revised structure of earnings. But this time their efforts were overshadowed by those of a number of newly formed groups. Some, like the Student Nurses Association represented specific interests, while others sought trade union unity behind their demands. Without doubt the most important influence upon the actions of the unions and the RCN was the meteoric rise of a new organisation known as the United Nurses Association. This organisation rejected the union's help and considerably embarrassed the RCN by adopting a wholly militant stance in place of the more normal appeal to public sympathy. It threatened but did not conduct a strike of nurses, though it held several short sit-ins in public places throughout the country. Ultimately the government, again acting through management, offered a 22 percent across-the-board increase spread over a two-year period.

This offer came at a time when the government was attempting to check the explosive increase in pay demands following the end of statutorily imposed incomes restraints and is all the more significant for that. While the government was undoubtedly influenced by rising quit-rates among nurses, the campaign waged by the United Nurses Association gained a great deal of general support rather than alienating the public as had been feared by the RCN. Even at its peak the Association contained only a small percentage of Health Service nurses, but its impact has been much wider. A few months after the new agreement NUPE lodged a claim for another rise of 15 percent for nurses for which it achieved staff side backing. There is little chance of the claim being seriously entertained by management but it may represent the first of a new series of competitive bids for membership by staff side organisations.

There seems no hope of unity on the staff side of most of the functional Whitley councils without the "transfer of engagements" between unions in the Health Service and the acceptance of the union's role by the professional associations. Theoretically there seems little reason why training and qualifying new entrants could not provide a sufficient role for professional associations who might then develop their links with the unions in order to protect the remuneration, working conditions, and career opportunities of their members. The ideological resistance to such a strategy is immense. Unless one of the unions can increase its membership within the appropriate profession, as NALGO, ASTMS, and some other unions have among technicians, it seems unlikely that such a dual strategy will come into being within the larger professions. Even among technicians these unions were assisted by the acquiescence of the professional institutes. It seems more likely that bodies such as the BMA and RCN will continue to evolve towards a negotiating role and that unless unions can offer a more professionally oriented service they will continue to be overshadowed by the qualifying associations.

THE REVIEW BODY ON DOCTORS' AND DENTISTS' REMUNERATION

For most effective purposes nonsalaried doctors and dentists have remained outside of the Whitley machinery. Since 1962 the main fees and allowances have been determined in accordance with the recommendations of a standing review body set up on the advice of the Royal Commission on Doctors' and Dentists' Remuneration 1957-1960 "to advise the Prime Minister on the remuneration of doctors and dentists taking part in the National Health Service." The criteria used in its awards right up to the twelfth one made in June 1970 were fixed in 1946 by the Committee on the Remuneration of General Practitioners (Spens) and similar ad hoc review bodies related to dentists, consultants, and specialists set up by the government in the same year. These bodies laid down the principle that the real value of incomes received by these occupations in 1939 were to remain the benchmarks for their future salary levels. The method by which each doctor's remuneration is assessed is extremely complex and the application of intertemporal comparisons is therefore equally difficult.

As was explained earlier, general practitioners are paid a capitation allowance on each patient on their lists (with a statutory limit to the size of list upon which the NHS pays allowances). A central pool was set up in 1948 and financed from the Exchequer (consolidated fund). The size of the fund is calculated by reference to a national average net income times the number of general practitioners under the age of seventy. To this is added an amount for expenses which up to 1965 was again based on an average taken on a sample of income tax returns. Up to that year a number of allowances and deductions were made from the fund which had the effect of increasing the comparative advantage enjoyed by general practitioners who were doing consultancy and specialist work for other parts of the service, or who were incurring heavy capital expenses or undergoing graduate training: that is to say these individual costs were spread over all those participating in the fund. As a result of reforms put forward by the BMA in 1965 and implemented in subsequent review body awards, a system of direct allowances or loans has been introduced which reduces the levelling-out effect of the pool in some directions and provides greater weighting towards practitioners in difficult practices. However, the workings of the pool system make the translation of percentage increases in remuneration a less direct operation than it is in the salaried sector and is in itself a source of frustration among many doctors.

167

In his acceptance of the Spens criteria the minister made it clear that he retained the right to amend or veto the awards of review bodies. The Royal Commission Report suggested that "while the government cannot abrogate its functions and responsibilities for ultimate decisions, we are insistent that the recommendations of the review body must only very rarely and for the most obviously compelling reasons be rejected" (para. 14). In the same report the commission fully recognised that pay increases recommended by the standing review body might have "repercussions in other fields" but felt that it would be "quite wrong for them (the review body) to revise their recommendations because of the possible cost" to these.

In 1966 the review body (Kindersley) recommended an increase amounting to 33.3 percent overall which restored the eroded differentials of senior physicians. But its implementation was phased over the first year of the Prices and Incomes Act. Further awards of the review body were implemented in 1968 and 1969, awards in which demands for overtime payments for junior hospital doctors were turned down. In May 1970 the review body recommended another increase of 30 percent based on a new survey of earnings in comparative occupations over the period 1955-68, in which they referred to 1939 in their choice of analogues. The minister at first postponed publication of the report, then offered senior doctors a backdated 15 percent increase while approving the full 30 percent for young hospital physicians. The other half of the award to practitioners was referred to the Prices and Incomes Board for a second opinion. The BMA responded by organising a withdrawal of the services of general practitioners to the extent of refusing to sign medical certificates for patients requiring evidence of incapacity for work. For two weeks some 77 percent of doctors and dentists (BMA figures) withdrew their cooperation in respect to the administrative requirements of the service. At the same time ·the review body resigned en bloc saying that they regarded the government reference of their award to the Prices and Incomes Board as marks of no confidence in themselves personally and as undermining the position of the body.

The dispute coincided with a general election campaign and the return of a new government enabled the BMA to resume negotiations with another minister. The Secretary of State withdrew the reference from the board but could not prevent the publication of a scathing attack on the statistical basis of the arguments put forward by the BMA and accepted by the review body. The minister agreed to an award amounting to an additional 5 percent for doctors and dentists which the BMA accepted in the light of "the new understanding given to them of the gravity of the economic situation." The chairman and committee members of the review body agreed to resume their duties.

It is highly likely that a Labour administration would have made the pay of doctors and dentists the subject of the standing reference to the NBPI, as with the armed services. The result of the dispute must throw further doubt on the ability of badly serviced bodies of part-time nonspecialists to review salary movements and to make awards on the basis of data which they are not in the position to investigate or to challenge. In the short term the dispute further widened the gap between the BMA and the Junior Doctors Association. The latter were willing to make common front with the former during the delayed publication of the report but condemned the withdrawal of practitioners services after the award. For different reasons the Royal Colleges also condemned the BMA's action while condemning the government's reference to the NBPI. In the longer term the dispute has probably served to dissipate some of the public sympathy upon which the profession formerly based its negotiating strategy, and also served to align it with the more militant Medical Practitioners Union (now part of ASTMS).

DISPUTE SETTLEMENT

The constitution of the Whitley Councils specifies that where it is impossible to reach decision on any subject "it shall be open to the management *or* the staff organisations concerned to seek arbitration in accordance with terms of an arbitration agreement to be determined by the general council." The interpretation of this clause is one that has been the subject of considerable controversy. It has been argued by management that to allow unfettered recourse to arbitration might lead to pronouncements on issues of principle with long term effects which were unacceptable to management. In this case subsequent government action to quash the award would be required, a ministerial right which was written into the 1946 act.

As a result of this management stand taken in the early days of the Health Service a special board of arbitration has never been appointed. On the suggestion of management the Industrial Court has become the chief arbitration body for the NHS and has been "encouraged to specialize in Health Service arbitration." The subsequent establishment of separate arbitration machinery in other parts of the public sector and of a police council which provides arbitration at the request of either party, proved a temporary embarrassment to management side in 1953; they nevertheless refused to change their views.

This was not of serious consequence to staff side until 1959. Up to that year it was possible for them to resort to the Industrial Disputes Order of 1951 which embodied the wartime right of unilateral recourse to arbitration in what appeared to be a permanent form. When faced with the refusal of management to allow resort to the Industrial Court, the staff side, in particular the unions on the Ancillary Council and on Administrative and Clerical Council, often referred disputes to the National Arbitration Tribunal (NAT), a quite separate structure of local tribunals. The latter were the first actually to take a claim to the NAT in 1950 and thereafter of fifty-five claims made in that council up to 1964, sixteen went to arbitration, a great many before 1959. In that year the power of unilateral application was effectively abolished for public service unions by the Terms and Conditions of Employment Act.

Staff sides in other councils have made little use of the Industrial Court, and generally their professional members prefer the ad hoc committee of investigation or review which considers all aspects of recruitment and career development within the occupations covered by the functional council. This is the case with nurses and midwives in spite of a successful reference in 1962 when after several months of parliamentary lobbying they had failed to elicit a pay raise of more than the 2.5 percent then prescribed under the "guiding light" (guide lines) policy of the government. At that time the Court awarded them the whole of the claimed 7.5 percent as an interim raise and ordered management side to start negotiations for another increase immediately and to conclude an agreement within six months. The fact that no agreement was reached in the stated time and a second resort had to be made to the Industrial Court is perhaps one explanation for the little use of arbitration made by professional bodies. Indeed since the minister retains the absolute power of veto it may be said that the whole concept of arbitration has been devalued. In this context it may seem more attractive to seek direct negotiations with the minister's representatives wherever possible, especially where the substantive content of negotiation relates to fees rather than to wages or salaries.

As in other parts of the public service there are no conciliation procedures and with the exception of the standing review body for doctors and dentists and other ad hoc committees set up from time to time to investigate and recommend on recruitment and conditions in the appropriate occupations there is little outside invasion of the overall authority of management. A form of inquiry is that of the outside investigator or mediator appointed by the minister. Such an appointment was made in 1956 when the minister asked an academic (Sir Noel Hall) to investigate and report on a pay claim for administrative and clerical staff. He was appointed after the local representatives on management side had protested against the refusal of ministerial representatives to negotiate for six months during which they, as local employers, were losing staff.

This same incident led to the first use of the ministerial veto of a Whitley award, since the Whitley agreement which the minister subsequently refused to implement was regarded by management as the first instalment on the changed, and increased, levels of earnings suggested by Sir Noel Hall. This veto led on to one of the few nationally led actions taken by union members against the NHS. For five weeks staff side led by NALGO banned all overtime work by clerical and administrative workers. Despite the great publicity given to the action and a large amount of public sympathy engendered the action was somewhat abortive. An interim award was not finally obtained until an Industrial Court suggested it some nine months later and the Hall report was finally implemented in the modified form of a subsequent Industrial Court and about twelve months after the first.

The reason for this delay is basic to an understanding of staff relations in the NHS. Given that cooperation outside of narrow professional channels of communication is difficult to obtain, then conjunctional or adversary bargaining is much more normal than in the civil service or Post Office. This requires the use of effective sanctions: the withdrawal from overtime working by administrative and clerical workers should have been extremely effective during a period of staff shortages and tight labour markets. In fact it was not because clerical staff worked much harder than before in order to keep up with the work flow and thus prevented any detrimental effect to patients or other users of the health service. Small unofficial strikes among lower grade employees are infrequent, as are public demonstrations but they usually have a force of explosive frustration behind them which make their strategic control by national leaders somewhat difficult.

Doctors have developed a different strategic concept of the withdrawal of their labour. The BMA have on three occasions since the war organised lists of names of practitioners prepared to withdraw their services from the Health Service in support of their collective demands. The first in 1946 was not very successful, the second gained an interim pay award in 1956, and the third in 1965 was extremely successful both in terms of membership support and in its success in obtaining a change in the government's pay offer, and the acceptance of a "doctors' charter" relating to future pay and prospects. The basis upon which they equate professional ethics with the strike weapon depends upon their continued ability to serve the public on a fee-paying basis—their withdrawal being only seen in terms of their mass departure from the administrative structure of the NHS. In an increasingly affluent society this strategy is being seen as an attractive one by many general practitioners. The great expansion in employer-provided private health insurance among white-collar workers, including senior civil servants, has led to attempts by prominent members of the BMA to establish an alternative health scheme, a concept in which the association has itself shown considerable interest. A recent BMA council meeting considered a contingency fund designed to help bring an alternative type of service into operation in event of a mass withdrawal of general practitioners. Such action could result in a doctor or a dentist being sued in a civil action for breach of his or her individual contract. In fact the practitioners who took part in the withdrawal of services from administrative duties in June 1970 could also have been sued in the same manner. Needless to say no one was, and it seems doubtful whether such an individual sanction could be effective in a national withdrawal.

It is difficult to see how any other than a professional or self-employed group could adopt such a strategy, since any salaried or wage paid worker could hardly continue to give his services to the sick on a fee-paying basis. The former leader of the United Nurses Association, Sister Patricia Veal, has recently left the Health Service and has urged other nurses to join her in subcontracting their services to the Health Service and thus freeing themselves from the constraints of permanent contracts. While this form of nursing is becoming an increasingly attractive mode of employment it can however hardly escape from the monopoly market of the NHS in the manner that the higher professions can.

THE POLITICAL PRESSURE GROUP

All of the major unions in the Health Service are affiliated to the Labour Party and on a number of occasions their connections have been used with some effect in organising Parliamentary lobbies. Yet it is probably true to say that the

Royal College of Nurses and the British Medical Association have organised more tactically important lobbies from their formally apolitical position than have the trade unions. The BMA's experience of lobbying dates from its campaign to re-structure the 1911 National Insurance Bill, a task which it took up again in 1946. On the second occasion an attempt to organise a boycott of the NHS failed because of the extent of the support given to the scheme within the profession. As a result its parliamentary lobby was seriously undermined. Nevertheless it gained and has retained direct access to the minister in all negotiations, a privilege which releases it from the protracted processes of "custodial" bargaining in the Whitley machinery.

Both the BMA and Royal College of Nursing gain consider-able entree into the administrative processes of the Department for Health and Social Service by virtue of their interests in the training and supply of qualified manpower. Like the BMA, the Royal College of Nursing perfected its lobbying techniques early in the century during their attempts to obtain training facilities for nurses and the establishment of an independent, elected General Nurses Council. It used its powers to oppose much in the 1946 act that was regarded as threatening their predominance and succeeded in gaining a professional monopoly for the first time. In 1961 it took the lead in initiating debates in the House of Commons and in organising the subsequent mass lobby of M.P.s.

It remains to be seen whether the relationshhips enjoyed by the BMA and RCN within the ministry which have been based on a professional involvement in the work of administering the service can survive a progressive adoption of an aggressive stance in pay negotiations. It will be regarded by the present minister as a duty of first importance to restore these relation-ships to "normalcy."

GRIEVANCE PROCEDURE

Like that of the Post Office the Health Service Whitley machinery is supplemented by an individual grievance procedure or in the more common English parlance "a procedure for settling differences." It is extremely elaborate and provides the only link between the national Whitley Councils and the direct employers of NHS staff. An employee may in the first instance appear with his union representative (or alone) before his employing authority (usually the Hospital Management Committee) or previously before any subcommittee of that authority. He may then appeal, through his recognised professional association or trade union to a regional appeals committee. This committee is appointed from two panels, three from a management side panel, three from a staff side panel (four on each side for cases within the purview of the Ancillary Staffs Council). In neither can nominees on the ad hoc Appeals Committees be members or employees of the authority directly concerned in the appeal.

Ultimately, failing satisfaction at regional level, the employee's association or union may request that the appropriate functional Council shall hear and adjudicate on the grievance. Both joint secretaries have to agree that it should appear on the agenda of their Whitley Council; the hearing must be taken as early as possible and in any case within two months of their decision.

The appeal to the regional committee must normally be made within three months of the receipt by the employee of his local employer's decision, and the hearing within two months of its receipt by the management side. Employees must be represented by a representative of the appellant organisation and the case for the employing authority by the authority's representative, neither being lawyers appearing in a professional capacity. Witnesses may be called by either side and may be examined by the representatives of the appellant and employer according to the normal rules of court procedure. The procedure at national level is however that of discussion and decision by consensus in the normal Whitley manner. It is theoretically open to either party to refer the matter to arbitration if a "failure to agree" is recorded at national level. In practice, since the Industrial Court procedure has been the only one available since 1959, both parties have to agree to such references and management have shown themselves to be reluctant to do so.

Initially a great many problems were encountered in the interpretation of the agreement, especially in relation to disciplinary offences. Hospital management committees are the de facto employers of most regular staff with power to hire and fire. For many years the management side of the General Whitley Council have refused any right of appeal against disciplinary decisions taken at this level. It still remains true that such grievances cannot be processed through grievance procedure and indeed in most instances local representation in such cases is not very effective. The weakness of the union position in Health is reflected in NALGO's evidence to the Donovan Commission in which it suggests that (1) dismissed employees should be legally entitled to a written statement on the reason for their dismissal, and (2) an independent appeal board supervised by a public agency or a special labour court should be set up to hear dismissal cases.

Generally, managements have attempted to restrict appeal decisions to those which do not set major precedents and thus add to the substantive content of rules made outside the negotiating chamber. The staff side who use the machinery most have attempted to add to the authority of the procedure and to widen the content of the issues treated by it. These staff sides are of course those representing hospital staffs, but even among these staff the number of grievances dealt with in any year is infinitesimal compared to those processed in such machinery in most of the private sector.

In its primary effect the introduction of grievance procedures was most important to ancillary staff and to some extent to clerical and technical staff. For many professional workers the disciplinary powers of their professional council—in particular deregistration—is of greater significance than local disciplining within the work organisation. While this greater power is hardly likely to be exercised except in the case of some extraordinary misdemeanour it remains a latent threat behind the limited authority of a hospital matron or senior registrar. Use of the grievance procedure against a superior has a career significance which militates against its use for matters of short-term discomfort.

JOINT CONSULTATION AND THE ADMINISTRATIVE STRUCTURE

The realisation of the vacuum which existed in labour relations below the level of National Councils led to the creation of the grievance procedure and during the same period to the creation of hospital staffs consultative machinery. The Whitley agreement of 1950 is a curious one. It begins by laying down some basic rights for recognised staff associations and unions—use of a notice board for the publication of meetings and the granting of "reasonable" facilities for such meetings. It then sets out the model constitution and objectives for joint consultative committees of management and staff in all NHS hospitals where numbers are great enough. Such committees are to consist of members appointed by the management committee or board of governors to include both committee members and principal officers. Staff side is to consist of representatives of clerical, nursing, technical, domestic, and garden and artisan (craft) employees. The objectives include that of giving "the staffs a wider interest in and a greater responsibility for the conditions under which their work is performed." Subject to the proviso that no recommendations may conflict with any Whitley agreement, the consultative councils may deal with such matters as the distribution of working hours, holiday arrangements, physical working conditions, and the general interpretation of nationally agreed rules.

Clearly such scope would give shop stewards or local union agents immense power in an industrial manufacturing plant. At the present time there are few consultative committees meeting regularly in the NHS. Not many unionists feel the need for these bodies to say this is to beg the question of why this should be so. In themselves the creation of separate grievance and consultative procedures were major steps away from the all-embracing concept of Whitleyism, and might therefore be regarded as being symptomatic of the very different negotiating and administrative environments represented by Health Service as against that of the civil service.

Part of the reason for the lack of employee participation in local decision-making, either through the normal channels of bargaining or through the carefully prescribed consultative procedures, is the doubt that often exists as to who is making decisions on the management side. The object of a number of recent changes has been to attempt to clarify the local structure of management. In particular a report on the administrative structure and the character of nursing management (Salmon) has suggested greater coordination in practices and staffing between hospitals. These and other proposals are being implemented in pilot schemes at the present time and will go some way towards making staff consultation possible in a clear-cut decision making process.

CONCLUSIONS

The problems of the Health Service have a number of parameters which seem difficult to change in the short term. The Government's intervention in the Whitley process at every stage —from being present in negotiations to intervention in the final awards of the Councils themselves—has clearly led to some lack of commitment on the part of staff side. It has been suggested by NALGO, for example, that the service might be run as a direct service by the government and that staff-management negotiations should be with the Treasury. Certainly the history of the disputes over the lifetime of the NHS seems to display a willingness on the part of management to concede arbitration to staff sides after being particularly obdurate in resisting claims up to that point. It seems that the government has always been hypersensitive to increases in costs within the Health Services and particularly anxious to set an example here during any given form or stage of incomes restraint policy. In their attitude to negotiations in Health the government has also had an example to show to local authorities both in their bargaining within the service and for their own sector of employment. More particularly ministers have often felt compelled to protect the taxpayer against the board's willingness to pay the market rate for labour in order to keep up standards.

On the staff side the presence of professional associations, many of which are very firmly identified with a "management" view and whose members often fill senior administrative roles, makes unity with more traditional unions difficult if not impossible. That many of these professionals are working on a fee-paying basis is a further reason for strategic differences. The autonomy enjoyed by professional bodies in respect to the training and disciplining of their members places unions with narrower interests at a distinct disadvantage. On the other hand the lack of emphasis placed upon collective bargaining by senior members of the associations has seriously detracted from the negotiating strength of staff side. The views of such leaders have been at variance with those of their young members particularly with respect to the status of recent recruits and the basis upon which they should be paid.

The "doctrine of comparability" in earnings levels has been a difficult one to establish in the Health Service, largely because of the lack of outside comparisons. Professional bodies have attempted to make comparisons with the earnings of other professionals in private practice and the doctors have been allowed to refer to a fixed point in time when the market status of their occupation was possibly at its highest. Others, particularly nurses, have experienced difficulties which in part at least were the result of the strategy adopted by their leaders. At the present time their senior members are looking for comparisons among senior management rather than in the traditionally feminine professions. Hospital nurses have lagged behind most comparably qualified occupations. Nurses in the local authority service work alongside social welfare staff, many of whom receive higher scales of salary. These comparisons tend to create discontent, or, through superior placement on the nursing salary scales, tend to distort the existing earnings structure.

Ancillary workers, of whom most are domestics and clerical employees, have tended to relate their claims to those of civil service or local authority staff. For much of the postwar period union leaders hoped for some more formal link, first with the Tomlin criteria used in the civil service and then with the pay research exercises. Management have tended to refer to whichever group in central or local government work was lagging behind the other. The results have not been good for health employees; both the civil service and local authorities tend to lag behind the private sector simply through the time spent in the process of comparison. The NHS has therefore tended to lag even further behind the initial pace-setters in earnings in both aggregate terms and in the rate of increase of wages.

Coupled with the distinct pay disadvantages of NHS employees, the operation of grievance and consultative procedures compares unfavourably with that in other public services. Again much of the debilitations present within the procedural structure and attitudes towards them spring from the peculiar form of "professional administration," the nearest comparison to which might be the "craft administration" existing in some major traditional industries. The void at regional level is however one that has been carefully preserved by past administrations to avoid duplication in authority within the Whitley structure and to keep power in the hands of the minister.

The last Labour government proposed that the service should be decentralised to ninety health authorities, within which hospitals, general practitioner services and after-care provisions would be brought under a single managerial board. This suggested concurrent changes in the Whitley structure which could only have been beneficial. The authorities would have roughly paralleled a reorganised structure of local government so that many problems of relative authority on management side and comparability on staff side might have been solved. There would have been a real functional need for both sides to come together in new regional Whitleys. Claims based on changes in local working practices could be better negotiated within a more formal local structure and greater responsibility for such negotiations delegated to specific points in the system.

Perhaps as important would be the impetus given to the development of trained management, particularly in the personnel role. The introduction of an integrated medical-social service unit could lead to a decline in the authority of any one of the predominant interest groups present within the system at present. As the proposals stood, however, the area authority members would be appointed one third by the parallel local authority, one third by the professions and one third by the minister. Both of the major Health Service unions, NUPE and NALGO, submitted proposals for the participation of union representations in all local management committees. When compared with the civil service Whitley system these proposals do not seem so very drastic. It is probably the case that without some such imposed weighting towards the countervailing power of unionism the present state of industrial relations will continue into the future. While the present system may be seen as relatively satisfactory in containing most staff-management conflict over the past twenty-two years, this may have been because of the existence of beliefs and values which are in the process of change. A move towards reform in procedure taken now might serve to avert future conflict and/or demoralisation.

·VI·

General Conclusions

IN the recent consideration of British industrial relations
by a royal commission and innumerable other observers
little attention is paid to the negotiating machinery which has
been working with relative success in the public services for
many years. The last three chapters have attempted an analysis
of three of the four major areas of employment in which Parliament is the major source of finance (the other, education, is
dealt with in a companion monograph in this series by Professor
Harold Levinson). Despite the apparent efficacy of the negotiating machinery in these sectors there are a number of stress
points within the bargaining institutions and areas of change
in the substantive content of negotiations which are inevitably
leading to changes.

On the employer's side there are the varying problems of
triad bargaining involving two sources of finance, thereby split-
ting the employer's bargaining front. Another problem is that
of custodial bargaining, until recently only experienced in the
National Health Service and Post Office, but more lately resulting
in a national strike of local authority workers over the local
implementation of an agreement made in the National Whitley
Council. If such agreements made or implemented at plant or
establishment level are to become normative in the public services the responsibilities of national bargainers may become
greater rather than less.

Local bargaining and the dispersion of members also presents
problems for underfinanced, badly serviced union negotiators.
Union attempts to come to terms with a highly centralised well
defined industrial structure of organisation and managerial auth-
itory in the public services have been somewhat varied in
their success. The Trades Disputes Act 1927 served to impose
a narrow structure on the civil service and the Post Office
staff organisations. Yet the varied technological context of the
Post Office has produced many different work roles among employees and as many vested interests built up and destroyed
by the same rapidly changing technology. Some senior grades

182

have attempted to acquire a form of professional separation: it was partly for this reason that the new corporation encouraged the creation of a separate management association. But it was probably the "rationale of the bargaining table" that caused the Postmaster General to separate senior managers who would be the corporation's representatives in local and, perhaps, national negotiations from representatives of other employees.

This dilemma of management representation as employees has not really been solved in the Health Service. Among nursing and medical staff in particular the same professional associations represent every grade from the most senior staff to the new entrant, and, because of the nature of the service structure and purpose the associations have acquired large areas of responsibility which would be considered managerial in other industries. Taken at its most abstract, professional associations in the NHS have acquired many of the rights and all of the problems that would face British trade unions if they acquired the place in management decision-making which is currently being demanded by many of their leaders. In the context of such control by professional employees in the Health Service it might be useful to extend the degree of participation among manual workers. It is however clear from the workings of Whitleyism throughout the public services that the involvement of the kind of manual workers is no easy task. Moreover, the prior act of union membership has yet to be accomplished in a high proportion of cases.

THE AUTHORITY OF EMPLOYERS' SIDES

The role of the minister or his representatives in central bargaining in the public services, particularly in the health and educational services, is one which has led to considerable controversy in postwar years. There are two aspects to this controversy. One is that of the minister's relations with the Treasury. The other that of his role in respect to local authorities or local managerial boards where both are responsible for the finance of the services or for its administration. The imposition of prices and incomes policy has led to a number of references of both claims and Whitley agreements to the NBPI and to the delay or amendment of awards by the respective ministers during the evolutionary years. The policy of the last Labour administration was clearly directed at shifting the emphasis in the distribution of the national income towards capital expenditure and away from current consumption. Equally clearly their ambitions were not fulfilled in the private sector. Within the public sector, however, this emphasis has resulted in limiting wage and salary increases as the Treasury kept a very tight control on the real value of overall public expenditure. The pressures of capital investment have not yet played such a major part in the civil service budget, and the nonindustrial civil service Whitley staff side has throughout this period been negotiating directly with the Treasury. On the whole this has enabled negotiations to be concentrated in one place rather than in several interdepartmental battles. But much of the unanimity in civil service Whitleyism has probably emanated from a much closer identity of the Treasury spokesmen with the agreements to which they have actually been a party than with those made elsewhere by the management representatives of other departments. The increasing powers of the Department of Employment and Productivity in the administration of prices and incomes policy and the criticism of the quality of public service administration in the reports of the Prices and Incomes Board has perhaps weakened the strategic value of locating civil service management in the Treasury. Although the Treasury representative on the newly formed national Whitley official side is there "only as an ordinary Departmental member" it seems likely that his role will still be somewhat more important. In any case the new Civil Service Department will work very closely with the Treasury.

The question of shared responsibility on management side is most prominent in the Health Service Whitley Councils and in the National Burnham Committee for the negotiation of teachers' salaries in primary and secondary education. In the first case the dependence of most nonministerial representatives on management side upon government finance is absolute. Consequently their view of their representative in the Cabinet and in the decision-making process leading up to the budget is quite crucial; for much of the Conservative administration health expenditure along with other public expenditure was given less priority than at first had been expected. The demotion of the Minister for Health to non-Cabinet status for the early part of the last Labour administration was clearly regarded as significant by nonministerial members of NHS management. But from 1948 onwards the protracted negotiations in the NHS Whitley Councils have been seen by staff sides as the result of intragovernmental negotiations. For this reason they have constantly demanded Treasury representation on the management side, and NALGO has gone so far as to suggest civil service status for the Health Service.

A somewhat opposing view has been taken by the teachers unions and associations who comprise the teachers panel (staff side) of the national negotiating committee for teachers in primary and secondary schools (the Burnham Committee). These schools are administered by the major local authorities whose representatives make up part of the employer side of the Burnham Committee, representatives of the Department of Education and Science contributing a minority of "observers" (see Chapter II). The teachers have strongly objected to the presence of the ministry representatives, but have been even more incensed by the intervention of the minister (the Secretary of State for Education) on two occasions in 1961 and 1963 to reduce or redistribute awards under Burnham agreements. Later in 1969, the minister greatly offended the management representatives of the local authorities by intervening in a deadlock in Burnham negotiations. An impasse resulted which, according to the chairman, had been created by the minister's refusal to meet union demands which local authority representatives might have conceded.

CHALLENGES TO ARBITRATION

Clearly the minister's part in this duet on the employer side of NHS Whitley and the Burnham Committee is a crucial and highly sensitive one, particularly where, as in the latter case, local taxation accounts for a large part of the salaries covered by any agreements made within the Committee. In particular the action of the minister in setting aside arbitration decisions or virtually negating them by postponement in a period of rising prices, has had a significant effect on the value of this process. The refusal of the National Union of Teachers to go to arbitration last year is just one of the more manifest examples of this decline in status that the process of arbitration has suffered in other sectors of public service. This new lack of faith among unions is not of course wholly to their advantage. While arbitration is regarded as "compulsory" in most public service negotiating machinery (except Health) statutory means of preventing strikes have so far not been used. Such means exist, as in section 5 of the Conspiracy and Protection of Property Act 1875, but in practice this law has hardly begun to be tested. This is because of the inherent weakness of public servant unions in this regard; an abandonment of arbitration might therefore be regarded weakening their bargaining position unless replaced by some new form of sanction. It is perhaps for this reason that the editorials of union journals express themselves with such vehemence on what their editors see as the invasion of the arbitration process represented in the statutory prices and incomes policy.

Yet the trend towards the use of investigatory committees and the publication of detailed analyses of industrial relations disputes by the Prices and Incomes Board have probably had some influence in modifying the procedure of the Civil Service Arbitration Tribunal. It seems unlikely that either the growing ministerial interventionism or the trend to investigation by management consultants, government and private, will have a determining effect on the long term viability of arbitration in the public services. At the moment there is a log jam of inefficient practices, both management and labour restrictions which stand in the way of organisational changes suggested in the recent spate of government sponsored reports. The compromise solutions put forward by traditional arbitration has tended to legitimate and reinforce prevailing inefficient work practices. The NBPI and other investigatory bodies have tended to reveal this past weakness.

These bodies are themselves to be regarded as a somewhat transient means of achieving changes in attitudes on both sides of negotiations. If they are successful in their efforts this success will show itself in the changes within employing organisations such as the establishment of the Civil Service Department and of the pilot introduction of Salmon-type management structures in some hospitals. Given that organisational changes include built-in efficiency audits and such consultative committees on technological change as those which exist in the Post Office, then arbitration should by virtue of the issues which arise assume a different and in many respects a more important role. It seems probable that local bargaining will become more important in most areas of the public service. Agreements made in such negotiations will often, like the present working out of productivity deals in local authorities, be made as a package— a complex combination of exchanges in work practice for modified rewards. The term "dispute of rights" is at present unknown in British industrial relations parlance; one suspects that, as in the private sector, in the public services also the emergence of closed-end formal agreements at local level will rehabilitate arbitration to adjudicate the working out of such agreements.

LOCAL NEGOTIATIONS AND THE PROBLEMS FOR REPRESENTATIVE ORGANISATIONS

Another major source of weakness or strength in the centralised public services is the relative lack of a recognisable grievance procedure at local levels. In both the Post Office and Health Service they exist on paper in an extremely elaborate form but, certainly since the early days of the Health Service when a whole spate of individual grievances went to arbitration, they are now relatively little used. This is also true in education, yet there seems to be plentiful evidence, some hearsay, some collected by breakaway or younger groups of employees, that the structure of authority in schools, hospitals, and to a lesser extent in the Post Office does go beyond that of the normal industrial line management. The positions of head teachers and matrons are imbued with a professional status and concomitant "infallibility" not normally claimed by an industrial line manager. This presents problems for the professional associations and unions aspiring to an "industrial" membership including both senior and junior grades. Indubitably much of the bitter resentment expressed by junior doctors, nurses, and teachers has stemmed from a discontent much wider and more fundamental than a concern with salary differentials. It has been displayed in a recent withdrawal by young doctors from the BMA and suggestions for independent hospital employment agencies for young physicians, to which the BMA replied with implied threats of deregistration.

The lack of use to which the grievance procedure is put may then be symptomatic of the nature of "line" management authority within these sectors of employment. This might also, as was suggested earlier, be an explanation of the apparent disinterest of nurses, clerks, and ancillary domestic staff in joint consultation with hospital management in the NHS. This is not to say that senior physicians, nurses, and teachers are necessarily authoritarian by nature. It may simply be that their vocational goals are seen as being more important than the inconveniences caused to their staff in attaining medical or educational success and the well-being of their "clients." Besides which of course since junior staff are "trainees," many can see no reason why new entrants to the profession should not "suffer as they suffered" in their early careers. In general, attitudes toward nonvocational staff of all kinds from administrators to domestics tend to be shaped by a similar vocationally centred view. The directors, that is to say the lay members of management boards in the NHS, as in education, often tend to be advised by members of the professions either from among their own senior employees or professional members coopted to committees, and they themselves tend to become immersed in the "conventional wisdom" of the professional bodies.

In the civil service the lack of formal grievance procedure has been made up by the ease with which individual grievances can be raised at local level outside of the Whitley machinery. But in the civil service as in all other public services the important characteristic of the grievance procedure has been that it has not been allowed to be used by the staff representatives as a means to extend the field of negotiable subjects *outside* of the Whitley Committees. That is to say that while in the civil service individual grievances are often settled outside of Whitley, as in NHS all final settlements with wide ranging implications have to be brought into national Whitley. In this way the public services have, so far, ensured the sanctity of agreements made at national level from the kinds of major extensions through local bargaining that have been made in private industry. Even in the Post Office most productivity deals relating to changes in local working conditions have been made in national negotiations for detailed working out at plant level. Hence it has been possible to retain control of nationally agreed rates and conditions from the central position occupied by the national unions and employers.

The recent negotiation of a similar agreement for local authority workers has led to a national dispute over the local implementation of the deal. The earlier strike of CPSA members in the Post Office related to the amount being offered nationally for changes in local working conditions. Clearly the unions are reluctant to give up their national bargaining strength for ad hoc local negotiations in which they are divided, competitive, and lacking in resources and expertise. Yet it is clear that employers are responding to government pressures and are attempting to develop management initiatives to organisational change at local level. The local structure of Whitleyism is particularly apt for this type of cooperative bargaining, but for the highly centralised public service unions this trend sets considerable problems in educating and servicing members. Already the dispersion of civil servants and the fundamental changes in working conditions and job definition resulting from the establishment of provincial computer centres has resulted in the build-up of full-time union staff.

Geographical dispersion is only one of the many pressures acting to change the structure of some public service unions. Dispersion of another kind, that of control over the financing of particular services and the consequent changes in status for the former public servant, has led some unions to expand outside their original field of recruitment into public corporations and beyond. The narrow base of civil service and post office unions has indubitably contributed to their effectiveness within the Whitley machinery and enabled evolution of staff side secretariat which reflects the ethos and interests of its whole membership. It was this kind of unity which appeared to have acted as a model for Dr. McCarthy's report on the ambulance men. The divided structure of Health Service bargaining (ambulance men and ancillary workers in residential homes are covered by the Local Authority Joint National Council) and the gulf which exists between the negotiating tactics of professional associations and those of the trade unions are such as to prevent any real staff side unity of interest in the Health Service even if the basis were present within the substantive content of the issues.

The principal success of Whitleyism has been in creating a context and commitment for "securing the greatest measure of cooperation between the State in its capacity as employer and the general body" of its employees that was seen by its architects as the main reason for its existence. Its failing has been that this machinery has only really worked in the manner in which it was intended to work and has existed at the levels at which it was intended to exist among nonindustrial civil servants, Post Office workers, and in a different form among senior and white-collar employees in the Health Service. Manual workers in the civil service, in the Health Service, and in local authorities are among the lowest paid in the country, and in spite of the national recognition of unions, union membership and union recognition in the full (American) sense of the term is extremely uneven from one public service establishment to another. In this market and negotiating context it is extremely difficult for management-staff consultation to develop on matters of long-term concern. The changes in the nature of their work content and reward structures now being put into effect may change this state of affairs as far as employee attitudes are concerned. Until the structure of union representation enables one union to speak for a majority of manual and domestic workers throughout the public sectors in the manner that the Post Office unions and the Civil Service Union speaks for manipulative grades, it seems unlikely that cooperative bargaining can be developed successfully among manual employees.

The future success of Whitleyism among professional employees depends upon the degree to which their associations will modify their attempts at unilateral job control and will be prepared to share decision-making with employers and trade unions perhaps even to develop dual strategies with the latter. The kinds of compromises and some of the trade-offs necessary to bring about a qualitative improvement in the nature of Whitleyism within the public services has been sketched out in the text. It may even be that Whitleyism could be extended further. In a period of increasing single employer monopsonistic control of labour markets there seems no reason why the Whitley structure should not in the future be extended to the private sector with hope of greater success than was obtained when it was first attempted fifty years ago.

Bibliography

CIVIL SERVICE

Journals of various civil service staff associations, particularly Civil and Public Service Association (*Red Tape*), the Society of Civil Servants (*Civil Service Opinion*), the Institution of Professional Civil Servants (*State Service*), the Inland Revenue Staff Federation (*Taxes*), and the Civil Service Union (*The Whip*)

Lord Fulton Committee, *Report on the Civil Service*, 1966-68, Vols. 1, 2, 3, HMSO, Cmnd. 3638; Civil Service National Whitley Council, *Developments on Fulton*, HMSO, February 1969; Civil Service National Whitley Council, *A Framework for the Future*, HMSO, March 1970; Evidence to the Lord Fulton Committee submitted variously by the Civil Service Clerical Association, the Society of Civil Servants, and the Institution of Professional Civil Servants, 1966-67

Campbell, G. A. *The Civil Service in Britain*, Penguin Books, 1955

Civil Service Pay Research Unit, Report for Survey Years 1966/67 and 1967 (unpublished)

Griffiths, J. A. G. "The Place of Parliament in the Legislative Process," *The Modern Law Review* 1951, vol. 14, pp. 279-96, 425-36

Humphreys, B. V. *Clerical Unions in the Civil Service*, Blackwell and Mott, 1968 CPSA, *Compendium*

Jennings, Ivor. *The Queens Government*, Penguin Books, 1960

Johnson, Nevil. *Parliament and Administration—The Estimates Committee 1945-65*, George Allen and Unwin, 1966

Mackenzie, Kenneth. *The English Parliament*, Penguin Books, 1950

National Board for Prices and Incomes, *Pay of the Higher Civil Service*, Report No. 11, HMSO, Cmnd. 2882, 1966

Reid, Gordon, *The Politics of Financial Control*, Hutchinson University Library, 1966

Walker, Geoffrey. *Pay Research in the Civil Service*, National and Local Government Officers' Association, 1968

POST OFFICE

Brown, D., and Howard, N. *The Future of Telecommunications*, Fabian Research Series 289, 1970

Civil and Public Service Association journal *Red Tape*

Civil Service Union journal *The Whip*

Frankel, S. J. *Arbitration in the British Civil Service*, Allen and Unwin, 1960

Hay, Ian. *The Post Office Went to War*, HMSO

Lerner, Shirley W. *Breakaway Unions and Small Trade Unions*, Allen and Unwin

Postal Departmental Whitley Council, written evidence to the Royal Commission on Trade Unions (unpublished)

Post Office Engineering Union. "Education in the Post Office," 1969; "Pay and Productivity Teach-In," 1968; "Evidence of POEU to the Royal Commission on Trade Unions and Employers Association," 1966; "75 Years—A Short History of the POEU," 1961

Post Office Management Staffs Association journal *The New Management*

Robertson, J. H. *The Story of the Telephone*, Pitman

Robinson, Howard. *Britain's Post Office*, Oxford University Press

Schneider, B. V. H. "The British Post Office Strike of 1964," Reprint No. 282, Institute of Industrial Relations, Berkeley, California 1966

Stagg, Norman. "The British Post Office Strike," *ILO Journal*, March 1969

H.M. Treasury. *Staff Relations in the Civil Service*, HMSO, 1961

Union of Post Office Workers: a) "How We Began" published by the union, 1960 b) Various issues of the union journal *The Post*

Various newsletters of the unofficial Telecommunications Operatives Union

Williams, Francis. *Magnificent Journey*, Odhams

193

HEALTH SERVICE

Abel-Smith, B. *A History of the Nursing Profession*, Heinemann 1960

BMA Year Book

Beveridge, William H. *Full Employment in a Free Society*, Allen and Unwin 1944

Bowman, Gerald. *The Lamp and the Book*, Queen Anne Press 1967

Clegg, H. A., and T. E. Chester. *Wage Policy and the Health Service*, Basil Blackwell, Oxford 1957

Eckstein, Harry. *Pressure Group Politics*, Allen and Unwin, 1960

Finer, S. E. *Anonymous Empire. A Study of the Lobby in Great Britain*, Pall Mall Press, London 1966

Government White Paper. *The National Health Service*, HMSO February 1944, Cmnd. 6502

Kahn, Hilda R. *Salaries in the Public Services in England and Wales*, Allen and Unwin, 1962

Kogan, Maurice. P. Draper, M. Kogan and J. N. Moore's "The N.H.S.—Three Views," Fabian Research Series 287, 1970

Ministry of Labour. "Industrial Relations Handbook," HMSO, 1964

National Health Service Act, April 1946, George VI

Vaughan, Paul. *Doctors' Commons—A Short History of the BMA*, Heinemann, 1959

Willcocks, A. J. *The Creation of the National Health Service— A Study of Pressure Groups and a Major Social Policy Decision*